A BIBLIOGRAPHY
OF PRINTED
BATTLE PLANS OF
THE AMERICAN
REVOLUTION
1775-1795

Published for
THE HERMON DUNLAP SMITH CENTER
for the History of Cartography at the
Newberry Library

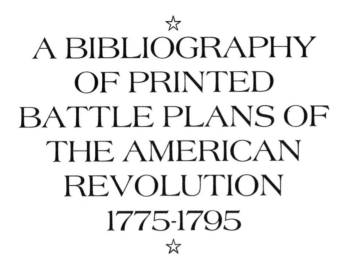

★
A BIBLIOGRAPHY OF PRINTED BATTLE PLANS OF THE AMERICAN REVOLUTION 1775-1795
★

Kenneth Nebenzahl

THE UNIVERSITY OF CHICAGO PRESS
Chicago and London

KENNETH NEBENZAHL is an internationally recognized authority on rare books and maps and president of a firm specializing in the sale of rare books and maps relating to America. He has published a number of articles and is co-author of the *Atlas of the American Revolution*.

The University of Chicago Press, Chicago 60637
The University of Chicago Press, Ltd., London

Library of Congress Cataloging in Publication Data

Nebenzahl, Kenneth, 1927–
   A bibliography of printed battle plans of the
American Revolution, 1775-1795.

   Bibliography: p.
   Includes index.
   1.   United States—History—Revolution, 1775–1783
—Maps—Bibliography.   I.   Title.
Z6026.H6N33   016.912′1′97333   74–16679
ISBN 0–226–56958–6

CONTENTS

PREFACE

This bibliography lists and describes the battle plans of the American War of Independence published between 1775 and 1795. It begins with I. De Costa's map of the Boston area, which depicts the engagements at Lexington and Concord where the first confrontation of military units took place. The work provides descriptions of each of the more than two hundred printed maps that followed, culminating in the plans of Charles Stedman. Included are maps issued as separate broadsides or published in atlases, books, pamphlets, almanacs, and magazines on both sides of the Atlantic.

The study is concerned with printed plans and does not include manuscripts. These printed maps, based upon the observations of eyewitnesses and published close to the time of the events that they help to describe, influenced large numbers of interested persons and helped to interpret what transpired. Just as De Costa's map was the first graphic representation of the epoch-making encounters of 19 April, 1775, many of the plans published subsequently were the earliest, and sometimes the only pictorial portrayals of revolutionary war engagements. To a public eager for news of the "rebel uprising" and His Majesty's forces thousands of miles away in the colonies, where in many cases relatives and friends were involved, these engravings were the equivalent of the instantaneous photo-journalism that has become customary in recent years. For example, to a Londoner in 1776, having available for sale in London a plan and explanation of a major British defeat at Sullivan's Island, South Carolina, six weeks after the action took place, when merely crossing the ocean could take from five weeks to three months, would have been comparable to today's television accounts via satellite from far-off battlefields.

Some were published with less speed, such as those issued after the war while controversies still raged over the causes and results of events. The terminal date of 1795 coincides with the publication of the German translation of Stedman's *History of the American War*, with its fine plans, which had first appeared the previous year in London. This was the final group of maps to be issued in the eighteenth century that were associated with participants. Stedman, a native of Philadelphia and an alumnus of William and Mary, was a young loyalist who was appointed commissary to the troops under Sir William Howe and served throughout the war. His *History* is considered, in England at least, to be the standard contemporary work on the subject. Earlier, other British commanders had published narratives of their roles in the war. Often, as in the cases of John Burgoyne, Banastre Tarleton, and John Graves Simcoe, their accounts were accompanied by important maps that are described in the present work. The battle plans of the American Revolution that appeared during the subsequent one hundred and eighty years were and are today prepared by historians or historical cartographers rather than eyewitnesses. Often the maps first brought together and described in this study are among the original sources relied upon by these historians and mapmakers.

The criterion in common among the maps included here is that they contain military information. Usually they are large-scale plans of small areas, although even those of the most significant and prolific publishers of them, William Faden, vary greatly in treatment. They are distinguished by the inclusion of symbols to indicate troop deployment, often in successive positions, and lines of march. Fortifications and ships that participated in the action are shown when appropriate, frequently with the lines of fire of their guns. Important topographical features are emphasized. General maps of large areas, prepared on a comparatively small scale and indicating the location of a battle solely by a symbol such as crossed swords, have not been included.

As in military confrontations throughout history, the terrain upon which the engagements were fought often influenced the tactics employed by the commanders, and thus contributed greatly to the outcome. The large scale on which most of the detailed plans were drawn allowed the cartographer to emphasize the relationship of hills, bluffs, ravines, lakes, rivers and streams, marshy lowlands, and coastlines with the positions taken up by defenders and the routes used by the attackers. From this viewpoint, the maps are as enlightening to the modern scholar as they were to the reader of the revolutionary period.

The science of military topographical engineering, and the art of mapmaking based upon it, had been developed to a very high degree by 1775. The best surveyors and cartographers in America at that time were military engineers stationed in this theater, and they contributed to the production of an accomplished cartographic genre. Of course, not all of the published maps were of the same graphic quality or accuracy. Some of them were wholly original; others were shamelessly derivative. The simpler and occasionally primitive delineations that appeared in popular publications such as almanacs and weekly magazines are also included.

Several of the maps appeared in more than one edition, generally an indication that they were avidly sought, not only by the government and the military, but by the public as well. In some cases the same plate was reworked several times to revise the location of the troops as movements progressed. Maps from the "theatre of war in America" represented a substantial business for the London map trade, although American, French, German, Dutch, Swedish, and Irish publishers were involved to some extent.

This study is an outgrowth of the research for a facsimile atlas of original battle plans of the American revolutionary war recently published by Rand McNally & Company. A thorough review was made of the basic bibliographical tools listed at the end of this volume, and the following map collections were systematically examined: the Newberry Library, the William L. Clements Library, the Library of Congress, the New York Public Library, the New-York

Historical Society, the John Carter Brown Library, and the American Antiquarian Society. Specific items were located in other institutional and private collections. At least one copy of each map has been examined. No attempt has been made to compile a census of extant copies, but the example used for purposes of the description has been noted.

Method of arrangement and description. The entries are arranged by theater of action and chronologically within each theater. Each area of conflict is introduced in the order of the date of its first battle; other engagements in the same area then follow in time sequence. For example, following the map of Lexington and Concord are all the other maps of New England actions. Then the scene changes to the Quebec-Albany arena, from the siege of Quebec through Burgoyne's surrender at Saratoga. Next, with the 1776 Charleston expedition of Henry Clinton, the Carolinas and Georgia are introduced, and the later engagements in those provinces follow the Charleston affair. In this way it is possible to present the various campaigns with a continuity that is not otherwise obtainable.

Maps that show more than one military event are entered under the campaign or action they illustrate most thoroughly. Cross-references are provided at the beginning of each battle section to maps in other sections that also provide some coverage of that battle.

The map descriptions themselves follow, with some variations, the principles outlined in the *Anglo-American Cataloging Rules* (Chicago: American Library Association, 1967). This work forms the basis of map cataloging practice at the Library of Congress, the New York Public Library, the Newberry Library, and in a growing number of other map collections in the English-speaking world.

The various parts of a description are discussed below in order of occurrence. Few entries in this bibliography make use of all the elements, but as many as are applicable to a given map are used in its description. The last four sections of the description (references, variants, copy described, and military information) are not a part of the

Anglo-American Rules but were added for this bibliography.

Title, authority statement, imprint. This information makes up the first paragraph of every description and may be assumed to be quoted directly from the map unless enclosed in brackets.

The full title of the map is given, following exactly the original wording and spelling, but not necessarily the punctuation. Typographical peculiarities such as the use of superscript letters or the long *s* are not recorded.

The statement on the map that indicates the person or persons primarily responsible for its production follows the title. The names of surveyors, cartographers, draftsmen, and engravers may appear here.

The place of publication, publisher, and date of publication are provided when they are stated on the map or can be determined from other evidence.

Size. Maps are measured in centimeters between the outer edges of the map border. Vertical dimensions are given first and all measurements are rounded up to the nearest whole centimeter.

Analytical note. If the map being described is part of another work (a book, a magazine, or another map), this is indicated here.

Scale. Map scales are given in the form of a representative fraction. The representative fraction, or RF, is a universal way to express scale. It indicates the relationship between *any* unit of measurement on the map and the same unit on the ground. Thus RF 1:15,840 means that one unit on the map represents 15,840 of the same unit on the ground. One inch on this map would represent 15,840 inches, or one quarter of a mile on the ground. To determine the number of miles represented by one inch on a map, the denominator of the RF is divided by 63,360 (the number of inches in one mile)—in the example above yielding .25 or one quarter of a mile. To determine the number of feet represented by one inch on a map, the denominator of the RF is divided by 12—using the same example, the answer would be 1,320 feet, or one quarter of a mile.

Note on source of title, authority statement, or imprint.

The source of information given within brackets in the first paragraph may be indicated here.

Physical description. Limited, in this bibliography, to the description of printed flaps or overlays attached to some of the maps.

Cartographic information. Maps are assumed to be oriented with north at the top; other orientations are indicated. Three methods of showing relief are found on maps described in this bibliography. The phrases used to describe them are: relief shown pictorially; relief shown by hachures; relief shown by shading. If a map of a water area includes soundings, the unit in which the soundings are expressed is noted. Maps that show lines of longitude are assumed to be based on the meridian of Greenwich; the use of prime meridians other than Greenwich is indicated.

Additional names. Information concerning persons associated with the production of the map who have not been previously mentioned is given here.

Contents. Important features appearing on or published with a map are briefly noted. These may include lists of references to the map, accompanying text, a dedication, or insets. The titles of all inset maps are given in brief form; those that show military information are provided with a separate description following the main map.

Sources and bibliographical history. This paragraph includes information regarding the sources of the map being described or its derivatives.

References. Works that supply more detailed bibliographical descriptions of the map in question are briefly noted. References to reproductions are provided for many maps. Full citations to the works noted here can be found at the end of the volume.

Variants. The descriptions in this bibliography are of the earliest known state of the map that includes military information (with the exception of a few maps from *The Atlantic Neptune,* the many early and possibly trial states of which were not examined). Many of the maps listed in this study were reprinted later after changes had been made to the printing plate. Where these *variant states* are known, they have been noted by briefly describing the changes or alterations or by giving a reference to a published bibliography. Differences between maps that do not involve changes to the printing surface (e.g., modifications in paper, letterpress text, or form of publication) are briefly noted, when known, as *variant copies*.

Copy described. Some of the maps described here are available in many research collections; a few are extremely rare. The location of the copy described has been noted. The library abbreviations used are as follows:

BL   British Library, London
DLC   Library of Congress
ICHi   Chicago Historical Society
ICN   Newberry Library, Chicago
KN   Kenneth Nebenzahl, Inc., Chicago
MiU-C   William L. Clements Library, University of Michigan
MHi   Massachusetts Historical Society
MWA   American Antiquarian Society, Worcester, Massachusetts
N   New York State Library, Albany
NHi   New-York Historical Society
NN   New York Public Library
RPJCB   John Carter Brown Library, Providence, Rhode Island
VHi   Virginia Historical Society, Richmond
VU   University of Virginia, Charlottesville

Military information. The final category is an annotation of the military content of each map. This usually includes a general assessment of the map and, as needed, notes on the depiction of topographical features, troops, fortifications, and ships. For the most detailed battle plans, further particulars are given regarding locations, deployment, movements and identification of troop units, number and size of cannon, and lines of fire of artillery and naval forces.

Acknowledgements. As in any work of this sort, the cooperation of many persons was required to bring the project to conclusion. It is a privilege to recognize them here. My wife, Jocelyn Spitz Nebenzahl, literally made possible this book and the atlas project with which it is associated. For the last four years she continuously provided the necessary inspiration to keep on with the work and cheerfully made many sacrifices, as it was done mainly in "spare" time.

Robert W. Karrow, Jr., Acting Curator of Maps at the Newberry Library, has been my research associate for the past two years. He brought to this bibliography a high degree of professionalism, surveyed many of the sources that led to the discovery of the appropriate maps, aided in the compilation of all the entries, the list of references, and the index, and generally provided the support without which the job would have been impossible.

David Woodward, Program Director of the Hermon Dunlap Smith Center for the History of Cartography at the Newberry Library and editor of the Center's publications, has given vital aid and encouragement. Lawrence W. Towner, Director of the Newberry, John Aubrey, and many others of the staff has been of great assistance.

Howard H. Peckham, Georgia Hough, and Douglas W. Marshall of the William L. Clements Library, the University of Michigan; Walter W. Ristow and Andrew M. Modelski of the Library of Congress Geography and Map Division; Thomas R. Adams, Jeannette Black, and Richard Boulind, of the John Carter Brown Library, Brown University; Georgia B. Bumgardner of the American Antiquarian Society; Gerard D. Alexander, Maude D. Cole, and Elizabeth E. Roth of the New York Public Library; James Gregory of the New-York Historical Society; Darrell Welch of the New York State Library; Joan St.C. Crane, Alderman Library, the University of Virginia; Alexander O. Vietor, Sterling Memorial Library, Yale University; Helen M. Wallis and Yolande O'Donoghue of the Map Library, the British Library; all have cooperated in many important ways. Merrily Smith has carefully typed the entire complex manuscript.

The errors and omissions are mine, and advice from readers regarding them will be sincerely welcome.

1

THE WAR IN
NEW ENGLAND

BOSTON CAMPAIGN   APRIL 1775–MARCH 1776
Lexington and Concord, Mass.   19 April 1775

1

A Plan of the Town and Harbour of Boston and the Country Adjacent, with the Road from Boston to Concord Shewing the Place of the Late Engagement between the King's Troops & the Provincials, together with the Several Encampments of both Armies in & about Boston. Taken from an Actual Survey. Humbly Inscribed to Richd. Whitworth Esqr. Member of Parliament for Stafford by His Most Obedient Servant I: De Costa. C. Hall sc.

London: I. De Costa, July 29th 1775.
37 x 49 cm.
Scale ca. 1:120,000.
Relief shown by hachures; soundings in fathoms.
Prime meridian: London.
Includes "references" 1–19.

References. Stokes and Haskell, p. 47. Reproduced separately by Yale University Library, 1963; in Fite and Freeman, no. 64; *American Heritage Book of the Revolution*, p. 113; *Atlas of the American Revolution*, no. 1.

Variants. This state of the plate shows "Castle I." in the harbor and reference no. 2 refers to "The Somers Man of War." A later state with the same imprint changes the wording to "Castle Wm." and "The Lively Man of War" and also adds the word "Fort" on Castle William. A third state is known with the imprint changed to "London, J. Hand, Decr. 6th 1775."

Copy described. DLC.

Military information. The first published map of the first battle of the war. Shows figures of regular troops and the militia firing from behind stone walls. Illustrates the return of Colonel Smith's detachment from Concord and Lord Percy's force from Lexington. A composite of military information, it also indicates by reference the site of the Battle of Bunker Hill, and shows by the symbol of clustered tents the encampments of the three divisions of the provincial army during the siege of Boston. There is evidence to indicate that De Costa (still unidentified) was aided in the preparation of this map by Captain Jonathan Carver (see Lee, p. 101).

Siege of Boston 19 April 1775–17 March 1776

2

A NEW AND CORRECT PLAN OF THE TOWN OF BOSTON AND PROVINCIAL CAMP. ENGRAV'D FOR THE PENNSYLVA. MAGAZINE. AITKEN SCULP.
   [Philadelphia, July 1775]
   27 x 19 cm.
   In *Pennsylvania Magazine* 1(1775): opp. 291.
   Scale ca. 1:16,000.
   Relief shown pictorially.
   Inset: [Environs of Boston] (see map 2a).

References. Wheat and Brun 238. Reproduced in Guthorn, *American Maps*, p. 7.

Copy described. ICN.

Military Information. Shows the British battery on the common and the fortification of Boston Neck.

2a

[ENVIRONS OF BOSTON]
   [Philadelphia, July 1775]
   11 x 12 cm.
   Inset on map 2.
   Scale ca. 1:125,000.
   Oriented with north toward the upper left.

Relief shown pictorially.

Military information. Indicates provincial lines opposite Gage's lines in Roxbury area, the American positions from Cambridge on the Charles River north to Winter Hill on the Mystic River, and forts and artillery positions.

3

[A CHART OF THE HARBOUR OF BOSTON COMPOSED FROM DIFFERENT SURVEYS BUT PRINCIPALLY FROM THAT TAKEN IN 1769 BY MR. GEORGE CALLENDAR, LATE MASTER OF HIS MAJESTY'S SHIP ROMNEY]
> [London]: J. F. W. Des-Barres, August 5, 1775.
> 72 x 104 cm. with attached letterpress sheet 79 x 55 cm.
> In J. F. W. Des Barres, *The Atlantic Neptune,* 4 vols. (London, 1774–82) 3: no. 16.
> Scale ca. 1:24,750.
> Title from attached letterpress sheet.
> Relief shown by hachures and shading; soundings in fathoms.
> Includes "references" a-i, l-p.
> Attached letterpress sheet contains "Nautical remarks and directions."

References. Henry N. Stevens, "Catalogue," no. 96d. Reproduced by Barre Publishers, no. 4.

Variants. Henry N. Stevens, "Catalogue," identifies five states of this map.

Copy described. ICN.

Military information. Shows British batteries, entrenchments, and fortifications in Boston and Boston Neck keyed to "references." The numbers and sizes of cannon are indicated. American fortified positions surrounding Boston are delineated but not identified.

4

MAP OF THE ENVIRONS OF BOSTON. DRAWN AT BOSTON IN JUNE, 1775

London: J. Almon, Aug. 28, 1775.
19 x 26 cm.
In *The Remembrancer*, 17 vols. (London: J. Almon, 1775–
84) 1: front.
Scale ca. 1:46,200.
Relief shown pictorially and by hachures.

Reference. Reproduced in Winsor, *Narrative and Critical History* 6:208.

Copy described. DLC.

Military information. Shows camp and lines of Generals Putnam, Ward, and Thomas, British fortification at Boston Neck, and the American lines at Roxbury.

5

EXACT PLAN OF GENERAL GAGE'S LINES ON BOSTON NECK IN AMERICA. ENGRAV'D FOR THE PENNSYLVA. MAGAZINE. AITKEN SCULP.
[Philadelphia, August 1775]
30 x 23 cm.
In *Pennsylvania Magazine* 1(1775): opp. 358.
Scale ca. 1:3,325.
Oriented with north toward the upper right.
On page 358 are thirty letterpress "References to the plate" with the note "This is a true state this day, July 31, 1775."
Served as the source for a map published in Dublin in November 1775 (map 8).

Reference. Wheat and Brun 237.

Copy described. ICN.

Military information. The letterpress account states that, using this map, "it will be easy to form a perfect idea of the manner in which the General hath blockaded the entrances into [Boston]." Shows fortifications, guard houses, floating batteries, cannon, etc.

6

THE SEAT OF WAR IN NEW ENGLAND BY AN AMERICAN VOL-
UNTEER, WITH THE MARCHES OF THE SEVERAL CORPS SENT BY
THE COLONIES TOWARDS BOSTON; WITH THE ATTACK ON BUNK-
ERS-HILL
London: R. Sayer & J. Bennett, 2 Septr. 1775.
46 x 54 cm.
Scale ca. 1:455,000.
Relief shown by hachures.
Prime meridians: London and Boston.
Insets: "Plan of Boston Harbour from an Actual Survey"
—"Plan of the Town of Boston with the Attack on
Bunkers-Hill" (see map 6a).

References. Stokes and Haskell, p. 47. Reproduced in Green,
after p. 44.

Copy described. DLC.

Military information. Troops marching from New Hampshire, Connecticut, and Rhode Island are shown converging
on Boston with artillery.

6a

PLAN OF THE TOWN OF BOSTON WITH THE ATTACK ON BUNK-
ERS-HILL IN THE PENINSULA OF CHARLESTOWN, THE 17TH OF
JUNE 1775
London: R. Sayer & J. Bennett, 2d Septr. 1775.
30 x 14 cm.
Inset on map 6.
Scale ca. 1:18,300.
Relief shown by hachures.
Includes lists of fires, wards, and "references" A-I, K-M.
This inset and the smaller "Plan of Boston Harbour"
above it are printed next to the main map from a sepa-
rate copperplate that has its own imprint.
Served as the source for maps in Murray's *Impartial His-
tory* (maps 30 and 32).

Military information. Shows Charleston in flames, the Battle of Bunker Hill with location of both armies. Locates British warships and pattern of their bombardment, also battery firing from Cornhill in Boston.

7

A NEW AND ACCURATE MAP OF THE PRESENT SEAT OF WAR IN NORTH AMERICA, FROM A LATE SURVEY
  [London, October 1775]
  29 x 38 cm.
  In *Universal Magazine* 57, pt. 2(1775): opp. 169.
  Scale ca. 1:740,000.
  Relief shown pictorially.
  Prime meridian: Ferro.

Copy described. ICN.

Military information. Includes eastern Massachusetts, Rhode Island, southern New Hampshire, and eastern Connecticut. "Bunkers Hill" and "Charlestown in ruins" are so indicated; "March of the Provincials" is lettered on two roads leading to Boston, and a "camp" is shown at Worcester.

8

EXACT PLAN OF GENERAL GAGE'S LINES ON BOSTON NECK IN AMERICA. ENGRAV'D FOR T: WALKER'S HIBERNIAN MAGAZINE
  [Dublin, November 1775]
  29 x 22 cm.
  In *Walker's Hibernian Magazine* 5 (1775): opp. 667.
  Scale ca. 1:3,425.
  Oriented with north toward the upper right.
  Letterpress on page 667: "From the Pennsylvania Magazine. . . . References to the plate [1–30]. . . . This is a true state this day, Sept. 31, 1775."
  Derived directly from a map in the *Pennsylvania Magazine* (map 5).

Copy described. MiU-C.

Military information. As on map 5.

9

FIG. 1. PLAN OF BOSTON
[New York, 1775]
8 x 15 cm.
In John Nathan Hutchins, *Hutchin's Improved: Being an Almanack and Ephemeris ... 1776* (New York: Hugh Gaine, [1775]).
Scale ca. 1:25, 350.
Oriented with north toward the left.
Relief shown pictorially.
Inset: "Fig. 2" [Plan of the Vicinity of Boston] (see map 9a).
Letterpress on facing page includes "references to the plan. Figure 1" A-I, K-Q.
Very similar to map 11.

Reference. Wheat and Brun 235.

Copy described. MiU-C.

Military information. Limited to inset (see map 9a).

9a

FIG. 2 [PLAN OF THE VICINITY OF BOSTON]
[New York, 1775]
7 x 7 cm.
Inset on map 9.
Scale ca. 1:126,720.
Oriented with north toward the left.
Relief shown by hachures.
Keyed to references on facing page of text, "Figure 2" A-I, K-U.

Military information. Shows the lines of the Continental Army.

10

PLAN OF BOSTON
[New York, 1775]
14 x 8 cm.

In *The New-York and Country Almanack for . . . 1776*
(New York: Shober and Loudon [1775]).
Scale ca. 1:126,720.
Relief shown pictorially.
Includes "references to the plan" on verso, A–I, K–Z, 1–3.

Reference. Wheat and Brun 236.

Copy described. MWA.

Military information. Shows the lines of the American investment of Boston.

11

FIG. 1. PLAN OF BOSTON
[Norwich, Conn., 1775]
8 x 15 cm.
In [Benjamin West], *Bickerstaff's New-England Almanack for . . . 1776* (Norwich, Conn.: Robertsons and Trumbull, [1775]).
Scale ca. 1:25,300.
Oriented with north to the left.
Relief shown pictorially.
Inset: Fig. 2 [Plan of the Vicinity of Boston] (see map 11a).
Letterpress on facing page includes "references to the plan. Figure 1" A–I, K–R.
Very similar to map 9.

References. Wheat and Brun 240. Reproduced in Guthorn, *American Maps*, p. 37.

Copy described. MWA.

Military information. Limited to inset (see map 11a).

11a

FIG. 2. [PLAN OF THE VICINITY OF BOSTON]
[Norwich, Conn., 1775]
7 x 7 cm.
Inset on map 11.
Scale ca. 1:126,720.

Oriented with north to the left.
Relief shown pictorially.
Keyed to references on facing page of text, "Figure 2"
A–I, K, M–U.

Military information. As on map 9a.

12

TO THE HONE. JNO. HANCOCK ESQRE., PRESIDENT OF YE CON-
TINENTAL CONGRESS, THIS MAP OF THE SEAT OF CIVIL WAR
IN AMERICA IS RESPECTFULLY INSCRIBED BY HIS MOST OBE-
DIENT HUMBLE SERVANT B: ROMANS
[Philadelphia, 1775]
41 x 45 cm.
Scale ca. 1:317,000.
Relief shown pictorially.
Reportedly published by James Rivington and Noel and
Hazard (by Guthorn); printing variously attributed
to Nicholas Brooks (by Wheat and Brun), Robert Ait-
ken (by Evans), and James Rivington (by Guthorn).
Includes "A View of the Lines Thrown up on Boston Neck
by the Ministerial Army" with "references" 1–7.
Inset: "Plan of Boston and Its Environs, 1775" (see map
12a).

References. Evans 14444; Guthorn, *American Maps*, 41/3;
Stokes and Haskell, p. 48; Wheat and Brun 203, reproduced
after p. 124.

Variants. Stokes and Haskell report an earlier state, no
longer extant. Stokes's notes recording the variations are
also lost. Wheat and Brun record a later state (no. 204) with
legend symbols engraved in the margin outside right neat
line.

Copy described. MiU–C.

Military information. Limited to inset (see map 12a).

12a

PLAN OF BOSTON AND ITS ENVIRONS, 1775
[Philadelphia, 1775]

9 x 8 cm.
Inset on map 12.
Scale ca. 1:126,720.
Relief shown by hachures.
Includes "references" 1–12.

Military information. Shows Charlestown in flames, Bunker Hill, Breed's Hill with redoubt. "Provincial" and "enemy" lines indicated.

13

BOWLES'S NEW POCKET MAP OF THE MOST INHABITED PART OF NEW ENGLAND; COMPREHENDING THE PROVINCES OF MASSA-CHUSETS BAY AND NEW HAMPSHIRE, WITH THE COLONIES OF CONNECTICUT AND RHODE ISLAND, DIVIDED INTO THEIR COUN-TIES, TOWNSHIPS, &C., TOGETHER WITH AN ACCURATE PLAN OF THE TOWN, HARBOUR AND ENVIRONS OF BOSTON
London: Carington Bowles [1775?]
64 x 52 cm.
Scales ca. 1:800,000.
Relief shown pictorially.
Prime meridians: London and Ferro.
Inset: "Plan of Boston with it's Harbour and Environs" (see map 13a).

References. Stevens and Tree 32d. Reproduced in U.S. Navy Dept., *Atlas*, no. 3. Fite and Freeman, no. 60, is a reproduction of a later state.

Variants. Stevens and Tree identify three earlier and two later states. The earlier states are without the inset.

Copy described. DLC.

Military information. Limited to inset (see map 13a).

13a

PLAN OF BOSTON WITH IT'S HARBOUR AND ENVIRONS
[London, 1775?]
13 x 17 cm.
Inset on map 13.
Scale ca. 1:50,000.

Relief shown by hachures.
Includes "references" a-i, k-o.

Military information. Shows locations of entrenchments, batteries, and redoubts keyed to "references" that give details of number and size of cannon.

14

AN ACCURATE MAP OF THE COUNTRY ROUND BOSTON IN NEW ENGLAND, FROM THE BEST AUTHORITIES. ENGRAVED FOR THE TOWN & COUNTRY MAGAZINE
[London]: A. Hamilton Junr., Jan. 16, 1776.
32 x 42 cm.
In *Town and Country Magazine* 8 (1776): opp. 10.
Scale ca. 1:365,000.
Relief shown by hachures.
Prime meridian: London.
Inset: "A Plan of Boston and Charlestown" (see map 14a).

Copy described. ICN

Military information. Limited to inset (see map 14a).

14a

A PLAN OF BOSTON AND CHARLESTOWN, FROM A DRAWING MADE IN 1771
[London, Jan. 16, 1776]
32 x 12 cm.
Inset on map 14.
Scale ca. 1:22,500.
Relief shown by hachures.
Includes "references" A–I.

Military information. Shows "Liberty Tree" and "Encampment of the Kings troops" on the common.

15

A MAP OF THE TOWN AND HARBOUR OF BOSTON, DRAWN BY A CAPTAIN IN HIS MAJESTY'S NAVY
London: Publish'd . . . and sold at Spilsburys Print-shop, Feby. 7th 1776.

30 x 37 cm.
Scale ca. 1:80,000.
Relief shown pictorially.

Copy described. MHi.

Military information. Shows "provincial lines," "Genl. Gages lines," forts, and batteries.

16

A PLAN OF BOSTON AND ITS ENVIRONS SHEWING THE TRUE SITUATION OF HIS MAJESTY'S ARMY AND ALSO THOSE OF THE REBELS. DRAWN BY AN ENGINEER AT BOSTON, OCTR., 1775. EN-GRAV'D BY JNO. LODGE FROM THE LATE MR. JEFFERYS
London: Andrew Dury, 12th March 1776.
46 x 65 cm.
Scale ca. 1:14,900.
Oriented with north toward the upper right.
Relief shown by hachures.
"To the public. The principal part of this plan was sur-vey'd by Richard Williams Lieutenant at Boston . . ."
Includes "reference" A–I, K–M, and 4 lines of "explana-tion."

References. Reproduced in *North American City Plans,* no. 5; *Atlas of the American Revolution,* no. 5.

Copy described. MiU-C.

Military information. Fine plan for illustrating the relation-ships of Dorchester and Charlestown Heights with the town of Boston. Shows troops (identified by unit) deployed in the city, and batteries, details of which appear in the "refer-ence." Particulars of the Battle of Bunker Hill and after-math are included. American fortifications encircling Boston are carefully drawn and explained. A note indicates that British works are colored green and rebel works yellow.

17

BOSTON AND THE ADJACENT COUNTRY WITH THE STATIONS OF THE BRITISH & PROVINCIAL ARMIES
[London, April 1776]

19 x 23 cm.
In *General Magazine* 1 (1776): opp. 150.
Scale ca. 1:43,200.
Oriented with north toward the upper right.
Relief shown by hachures.
Includes "references" a-i, k-p, NB.

Copy described. MiU-C.

Military information. Shows location of American units, particulars of Battle of Bunker Hill.

18

CARTE DU PORT ET HAVRE DE BOSTON AVEC LES CÔTES ADJA-CENTES, DANS LAQUEL ON A TRACÉE LES CAMPS ET LES RE-TRANCHEMENS OCCUPÉ, TANT PAR LES ANGLOIS QUE PAR LES AMÉRICAINS. DEDIÉE ET PRESENTÉE AU ROI PAR . . . LE CH'DE DE BEAURAIN, EN 1776. GRAVÉ P. CROISEY
Paris [1776]
56 x 70 cm.
Scale ca. 1:25,000 (not 1:25,000,000 as indicated by graphic scale).
Relief shown by hachures; soundings in fathoms.
Includes references A–M.
"Cette carte à été copié sur un plan original apporté à la cour d'Angleterre."
Reduced from a later state of The *Atlantic Neptune* map (map 3).
Served as the source for a German map of the same year (map 19).

Reference. Reproduced in Library of Congress, *Quarterly Journal* 30 (1973): 252–53.

Copy described. MiU-C.

Military information. An unusually fine topographic map, with elaborately engraved hachures. References are to number and caliber of artillery and locations of troops. The British and American units are shown in considerable detail (American first corps at Cambridge, second corps opposite Charlestown Neck, third corps above Roxbury).

19

CARTE VON DEM HAFEN UND DER STADT BOSTON MIT DEN
UMLIEGENDEN GEGENDEN UND DER LAGERN SOWOH DER AMER-
ICANER ALS AUCH DES ENGLANDER, VON DEM CHEVAL DE BEARIN
NACH DEM PARISEN ORIGINAL VON 1776. G. F. I. FRENTZEL
SCULPS.
    Leipzig: Johann Carl Müller, [1776]
    51 x 61 cm.
    From *Geographische Belustigungen zur Erläuterung der
        neuesten Weltgeschichte.* Stück 1. (Leipzig: J. C. Mül-
        ler, 1776).
    Scale ca. 1:25,000 (not 1:25,000,000 as indicated by
        graphic scale).
    Relief shown by hachures; soundings in fathoms.
    Includes "Erklærung der Buchstaben" A–C.
    "Diese Carte von einen Englischen vor die Regierung
        aufgenomnen Originale copiret worden."
    Derived directly from the map by Beaurain (map 18).

Copy described. DLC.

Military information. As on map 18.

20

A PLAN OF BOSTON IN NEW ENGLAND WITH ITS ENVIRONS,
INCLUDING MILTON, DORCHESTER, ROXBURY, BROOKLIN, CAM-
BRIDGE, MEDFORD, CHARLESTOWN, PARTS OF MALDEN AND CHEL-
SEA; WITH THE MILITARY WORKS CONSTRUCTED IN THOSE
PLACES IN THE YEARS 1775 AND 1776. ENGRAV'D IN AQUA TINTA
BY FRANCIS JUKES
    London: Henry Pelham, June 2d, 1777.
    98 x 70 cm.
    Scale ca. 1:14,100.
    Oriented with north toward the upper right.
    Includes facsimile of pass issued by James Urquhart,
        "Town Major," to allow free passage of Henry Pelham
        "to take a plan of the town's of Boston & Charlestown
        and of the rebel works round those places"; and "refer-
        ences to Boston" A–I, K–Q.

Dedication: "To . . . Lord George Germain . . . by . . . Henry Pelham" (autograph signature).

Reference. Stokes and Haskell, p. 49, Reproduced in Winsor, *Memorial History*, 3: after p. vi.

Copy described. DLC.

Military information. Very good and extensive information including British and American fortifications in Charlestown and in and about Boston, with their lines of fire.

21

BOSTON, ITS ENVIRONS AND HARBOUR, WITH THE REBELS WORKS RAISED AGAINST THAT TOWN IN 1775. FROM THE OBSERVATIONS OF LIEUT. PAGE OF HIS MAJESTY'S CORPS OF ENGINEERS, AND FROM THE PLANS OF CAPT. MONTRESOR
[London]: Engraved & publish'd by Wm. Faden, 1st Octr. 1777.
45 x 63 cm.
Scale ca. 1:24,000.
Relief shown by hachures; soundings in fathoms and feet.

References. Stevens and Tree 7A(a). Reproduced separately by Historic Urban Plans.

Variants. Stevens and Tree identify two later states. Both have the right hand border line cut away and extra half sheet added (making the horizontal dimension 86 cm.) and the year of publication changed to "1778." The latest state alters the title and adds a note.

Copy described. DLC.

Military information. Shows fortifications and troop locations with emphasis on "rebel lines" around Roxbury and Cambridge. American fortifications indicated on Dorchester Neck; on Dorchester Hill, "work begun."

22

A PLAN OF THE TOWN OF BOSTON, WITH THE INTRENCHMENTS &C. OF HIS MAJESTYS FORCES IN 1775. FROM THE OBSERVATIONS OF LIEUT. PAGE OF HIS MAJESTY'S CORPS OF ENGINEERS, AND FROM THE PLANS OF OTHER GENTLEMEN

[London]: Engraved & printed for Wm. Faden, 1st Octor.
1777.

45 x 31 cm.

Scale ca. 1:9,800.

Relief shown by hachures.

Includes "references to the lines &c" a-p, and "references
to the town" A–Q, 1–4; a note describes the battery
erected on Fort Hill by the Americans after the British
evacuation.

The manuscript engraver's copy of this map is in the
Library of Congress Faden Collection and is reproduced in Fite and Freeman, no. 62.

References. Reproduced separately by Historic Urban Plans;
in *Atlas of the American Revolution,* no. 2; Winsor, *Memorial History,* 3: opp. p. iv.

Copy described. ICN.

Military information. The most detailed town plan of the
period. Shows troop locations, batteries, the fortifications
of Boston Neck, headquarters of general officers. Identifies
troops by unit, and gives number and size of cannon.

23

BOSTON, WITH ITS ENVIRONS. ENGRAVED FOR DR. GORDONS
HISTORY OF THE AMERICAN WAR. T. CONDER SCULPT.

London [1788]

23 x 33 cm.

In William Gordon, *The History of the Rise, Progress, and
Establishment of the Independence of the United
States,* 4 vols. (London, 1788), 2: front.

Scale ca. 1:52,500.

Relief shown by hachures.

"Plate II. To face the title of vol. II."

Includes "references to Boston &c." 1–7.

Copy described. ICN.

Military information. The outlines and topography are
clearly reduced from the one-sheet version of Faden's *Boston, Its Environs and Harbour* (map 21) but a number of

military features such as locations of troops, batteries, and fortifications have been added.

Bunker Hill, Mass. 17 June 1775
See also entry: 1, 6a, 7, 12a, 16–17, 20

24

A SKETCH OF THE ACTION BETWEEN THE BRITISH FORCES AND THE AMERICAN PROVINCIALS, ON THE HEIGHTS OF THE PENINSULA OF CHARLESTOWN, THE 17TH OF JUNE 1775
   London: Jefferys & Faden, 1 Aug. 1775.
   35 x 31 cm.
   Scale ca. 1:14,000.
   Includes three columns of text.

Copy described. DLC.

Military information. The earliest published plan devoted wholly to the Battle of Bunker Hill. Shows lines of march and battle positions and the routes of the British ships and troop transports from the long wharf and north battery to their landing points at Charlestown. The text identifies the British regiments and commanders, describes Warren's redoubt, and gives particulars of the engagement.

25

[BATTLE OF BUNKER HILL]
   [New York, 3 August 1775]
   ca. 7 x 8 cm.
   In *Rivington's New-York Gazetteer,* 3 August 1775.
   Not constructed to scale.
   Oriented with north toward the left.
   Included to illustrate "Another Account of the Late Action at Bunker's Hill."

Reference. Reproduced in Frothingham, p. 397.

Copy described. MWA.

Military information. This is a very primitive typographical sketch constructed entirely from printer's rules and type. Shows "floating battery," rail fence, breastwork, etc.

26

THIRTY-MILES ROUND BOSTON. BY M. ARMSTRONG GEO. 14TH
AUGT. 1775. A BELL SC.
[Edinburgh, August 1775]
26 x 26 cm.
In *Scots Magazine* 37 (1775): opp. 440.
Scale ca. 1:390,000.
Relief shown pictorially.
Prime meridian: London.
Includes tables of "memorable occurrences" beginning
     with the Boston Tea Party and ending with the Battle
     of Bunker Hill.
Inset: "Action near Charlestown" (see map 26a).
"Price one shill."

Copy described. ICN.

Military information. Limited to inset (see map 26a).

26a

ACTION NEAR CHARLESTOWN, 17 JUNE 1775
[Edinburgh, August 1775]
11 x 10 cm.
Inset on map 26.
Scale ca. 1:100,000.
Relief shown by hachures.
Derived from the Jefferys & Faden plan of 1 August 1775
     (map 24).

Military information. Shows troop positions, dotted lines
labeled "troops landing" and "Provincials retreating to
Cambridge."

27

PLAN OF THE REDOUBT AND INTRENCHMENT ON THE HEIGHTS
OF CHARLES-TOWN (COMMONLY CALLED BUNKER'S HILL), OP-
POSITE BOSTON, IN NEW-ENGLAND, ATTACKED AND CARRIED BY
HIS MAJESTY'S TROOPS, JUNE 17, 1775
[London, September 1775]
9 x 10 cm.

In *Gentleman's Magazine* 45 (1775): p. 416.
Scale 1:1,800 or "50 [yards] to an inch."
Includes an eight-line explanation below the map.

Copy described. ICN.

Military information. This is a small woodcut plan of the
works, with inserted type. It shows a "strong wooden fence"
on either side.

28

A PLAN OF THE BATTLE ON BUNKERS HILL, FOUGHT ON THE
17TH OF JUNE 1775. BY AN OFFICER ON THE SPOT
London: R. Sayer & J. Bennett, 27 Novr. 1775.
35 x 35 cm.
Scale ca. 1:12,000.
Relief shown by hachures.
A copy of Burgoyne's letter to his nephew, Lord Stanley,
   describing the battle and dated 25 June 1775, is printed
   below the map.

Reference. Reproduced in *Atlas of the American Revolution*,
no. 3.

Copy described. DLC.

Military information. Shows landing of British troops, ad-
vance on the hill, rebel entrenchments, and Warren's redoubt. British ships and floating batteries covering the
invasion are depicted and named. Principal British batteries
on the Boston peninsula, with the number and size of guns,
are shown.

29

A PLAN OF THE ACTION AT BUNKERS HILL, ON THE 17TH OF
JUNE 1775, BETWEEN HIS MAJESTY'S TROOPS UNDER THE COM-
MAND OF MAJOR GENERAL HOWE, AND THE REBEL FORCES. BY
LIEUT. PAGE OF THE ENGINEERS, WHO ACTED AS AIDE DE CAMP
TO GENERAL HOWE IN THAT ACTION. N.B.: THE GROUND PLAN
IS FROM AN ACTUAL SURVEY BY CAPTN. MONTRESOR
   [London: William Faden, between 1775 and 1778]

49 x 43 cm.

Scale ca. 1:4,900.

An overlay (15 x 23 cm.) designated "No. 1" is tipped on at the right middle of the map and shows the first position of the troops. The map itself is designated "No 2."

Relief shown pictorially.

Includes "references to the plans. No. 1 [A–K] No. 2 [L–P, 2]" and note on reference "R."

Reference. Reproduced in *Atlas of the American Revolution,* no. 4.

Variant. A later state appears in Stedman's *History.*

Copy described. ICN.

Military information. The most detailed and informative delineation of this battle. The heights of Charlestown surmounted by Warren's redoubt, fences, hedgerows, deployment of defending troops, landing and lines of march of attacking forces, British ships covering the action, and the Corps Hill battery with lines of fire are all indicated. The overlay shows the initial attack that was repulsed, while the same area on the main map shows the later progress by the British up the hill to just outside the redoubt.

30

PLAN OF THE TOWN OF BOSTON WITH THE ATTACK ON BUNKERS-HILL IN THE PENINSULA OF CHARLESTOWN, THE 17TH OF JUNE 1775

Newcastle upon Tyne: Printed for T. Robson [1778]

29 x 14 cm.

In James Murray, *An Impartial History of the Present War in America,* 3 vols. (Newcastle upon Tyne: T. Robson, [1778–80]) 1: opp. p. 431.

Scale ca. 1:19,300.

Relief shown by hachures.

Includes a list of fires, another of wards, and "references" A–I, K–M.

Derived from the Sayer and Bennett inset of 2 September

1775 (map 6a); served as the source for a map in the Boston edition of Murray (map 32).

Reference. Reproduced in *American Heritage Book of the Revolution,* p. 106.

Copy described. ICN.

Military information. The battle is drawn as a tiny perspective view, with English forces charging the hill and "Charlestown in flames."

31

A PLAN OF THE ACTION OF BUNKERS HILL, ON THE 17TH OF JUNE 1775
   [London, 1780–81]
   47 x 49 cm.
   Apparently engraved for J. F. W. Des Barres, *The Atlantic Neptune,* 4 vols. (London, 1774–82).
   Scale ca. 1:3,900.
   Date from University of Michigan, William L. Clements Library, *Research Catalog* 3:88.
   Oriented with north toward the lower right.
   Relief shown by hachures and shading.
   Includes references A–I, K–U, W–Y.
   Although it bears no imprint, the style and technique of this plan clearly point to the engravers of *The Atlantic Neptune.* Not in Henry N. Stevens, "Catalogue."

Copy described. MiU-C.

Military information. Large-scale delineation showing troop positions keyed to references. Natural and man-made obstacles can be seen. Position of British ships and the British battery at Boston are shown with their lines of fire.

32

PLAN OF THE TOWN OF BOSTON, WITH THE ATTACK ON BUNKERS-HILL, IN THE PENINSULA OF CHARLESTOWN, THE 17TH OF JUNE, 1775. J. NORMAN SC.
   [Boston, 1781]
   29 x 16 cm.

In James Murray, *An Impartial History of the War in America*, 3 vols. (Boston: Nathaniel Coverly and Robert Hodge, 1781–84) 1: front.
Scale ca. 1:15,840.
Includes lists of fires, wards, and "references" A–I, L–M.
Derived directly from a map in the English edition of Murray (map 30).

References. Wheat and Brun 241. Reproduced in Winsor, *Narrative and Critical History*, 6:201.

Copy described. MiU-C.

Military information. As on map 30.

33

[PLAN OF THE WORKS ON BUNKER'S HILL, AT THE TIME IT WAS ABANDONED BY HIS MAJESTY'S FORCES ON THE 17TH OF MARCH, 1776]
[London, 1784]
18 x 23 cm. (to plate mark)
In William Carter, *A Genuine Detail of the Several Engagements . . . during the Years 1775 and 1776* (London: G. Kearsley, 1784), opp. p. 1.
Scale ca. 1:1,725.
Title from title page of book.
Relief shown by hachures.
Includes eleven lines of explanations.

Reference. Reproduced in Frothingham, p. 330.

Copy described. ICN.

Military information. A detailed ground plan, showing the perimeter, guard houses, gun emplacements, etc.

RHODE ISLAND   JULY 1778–JUNE 1781
Newport, R. I.   29 July–31 August 1778

34

A TOPOGRAPHICAL CHART OF THE BAY OF NARRAGANSET IN THE PROVINCE OF NEW ENGLAND, WITH ALL THE ISLES CONTAINED THEREIN, AMONG WHICH RHODE ISLAND AND CONNONICUT

HAVE BEEN PARTICULARLY SURVEYED. SHEWING THE TRUE POSITIONS & BEARINGS OF THE BANKS, SHOALS, ROCKS &C. AS LIKEWISE THE SOUNDINGS, TO WHICH HAVE BEEN ADDED THE SEVERAL WORKS & BATTERIES RAISED BY THE AMERICANS. TAKEN BY ORDER OF THE PRINCIPAL FARMERS ON RHODE ISLAND, BY CHARLES BLASKOWITZ

> [London]: Wm. Faden, July 22d 1777.
>
> 93 x 64 cm.
>
> In William Faden, *The North American Atlas* (London, 1777), no. 11.
>
> Scale ca. 1:50,500.
>
> Relief shown by hachures; soundings in fathoms.
>
> Includes "references to the batteries" A–H; "a list of the principal farms in Rhode Island" 32 names, A–B; and an eighteen-line note.
>
> Dedication: "To . . . Hugh Earl Percy . . . Wm. Faden."

References. Reproduced separately by Historic Urban Plans and John Carter Brown Library; in *Atlas of the American Revolution,* no. 16.

Copy described. ICN.

Military information. Ten batteries are indicated, number and size of cannon given in table.

35

A PLAN OF THE TOWN OF NEWPORT IN RHODE ISLAND. SURVEYED BY CHARLES BLASKOWITZ

> [London]: Willm. Faden, Septr. 1st 1777.
>
> 34 x 37 cm.
>
> In William Faden, *The North American Atlas* (London, 1777), no. 12.
>
> Scale ca. 1:6,100.
>
> Oriented with north to the left.
>
> Relief shown by hachures.
>
> Includes "references" A–T.
>
> Served as the source for a French plan (map 37a).

References. Reproduced in *North American City Plans,* no. 18; Winsor, *Narrative and Critical History,* 6:597.

Copy described. ICN.

Military information. Shows "a battery raised by the Americans."

36

A Chart of the Harbour of Rhode Island and Narraganset Bay, Surveyed in Pursuance of Directions from the Lords of Trade to His Majesty's Surveyor General for the Northern District of North America. Published at the Request of the Right Honourable Lord Viscount Howe, by J. F. W. Des Barres, 20th July 1776
> [London]: J. F. W. Des Barres, May 3, 1776 [i.e., 1778]
> 108 x 75 cm.
> In J. F. W. Des Barres, *The Atlantic Neptune,* 4 vols. (London, 1774–82) 3: no. 7.
> Scale ca. 1:51,000.
> Relief shown by hachures and shading; soundings in fathoms.
> Includes "notes and references explaining the situation of the British ships and forces after the 29th of July 1778 . . . July 30th . . . August 5th . . . 8th . . . 9th . . . ." A–I, K–L.
> Served as the source for a French map of 1778 (map 37).

References. Henry N. Stevens, "Catalogue," 86f. Reproduced by Barre Publications, no. 12.

Variants. Henry N. Stevens, "Catalogue," describes nine variant states of this map.

Copy described. ICN.

Military information. Shows positions of ships and encampments, locations of battle.

37

Port de Rhode Island et Narraganset Baye. Publie à la requête du Vicomte Howe par le chevalier des Barres, Londres 1776. Traduit de l'Anglais et augmenté d'après celui de Blaskowitz, publié a Londres en 1777

Paris: Le Rogue, 1778.

102 x 71 cm.

In George Louis Le Rouge, *Pilote Americain septentrional* (Paris, 1778), nos. 11–12.

Scale ca. 1:53,000.

Relief shown by hachures.

Inset: [Plan of Newport] (see map 37a).

Derived directly from a map in *The Atlantic Neptune* (map 36).

Copy described. DLC.

Military information. Limited to American fortifications of Providence and a few other forts throughout the bay.

37a

[PLAN OF NEWPORT]

[Paris, 1778]

21 x 34 cm.

Inset on map 37.

Scale ca. 1:6,336.

Relief shown by hachures.

Reduced from the Blaskowitz plan of Newport (map 35).

Military information. Shows a "batterie des Americains."

Rochambeau at Newport   11 July 1780–June 1781

38

PLAN DE LA POSITION DE L'ARMEE FRANÇAISE AU TOUR DE NEWPORT DANS RHODE ISLAND, ET DU MOUILLAGE DE L'ESCADRE DANS LA RADE DE CETTE VILLE. LEVE SUR LES LIEUX PAR LES INGENIEURS DE L'ARMEE

Paris: Le Rouge, 1782.

43 x 49 cm.

Scale ca. 1:23,155.

Relief shown by hachures.

Based on maps by Crublier d'Opterre, the Berthier brothers, or other engineers under Colonel Desandroüins.

Includes "Legende" 1–57.

Reference. Reproduced in *Atlas of the American Revolution,* no. 31.

Copy described. RPJCB.

Military information. Shows ships arrayed in harbor, lines of fire covering the entrance to the harbor from ships and batteries. Numerous troop locations and batteries shown on land. Represents French positions taken up by Rochambeau between July and September 1780.

PENOBSCOT EXPEDITION   JULY–AUGUST 1779
Penobscot, Me.   25 July–12 August 1779

39

TO THE RIGHT HONOURABLE LORD GEORGE GERMAINE ONE OF HIS MAJESTY'S PRINCIPAL SECRETARIES OF STATE &C, THIS CHART OF PENOBSCOT (REPRESENTING THE SITUATION OF ABOUT 700 OF HIS MAJESTYS TROOPS UNDER THE COMMAND OF BRIGR. GENERAL FRANCIS MCLEAN AND THREE OF HIS MAJESTY'S SLOOPS OF WAR COMMANDED BY CAPTN. HENRY MOWAT SENR. OFFICER, WHEN BESIEGED BY MORE THAN 3300 REBELS JULY 1779 COMMANDED BY BRIGR. GENL. LOVELL, AND SEVENTEEN VESSELS OF WAR COMMANDED BY COMMODORE SALTONSTALL), IS MOST HUMBLY INSCRIBED BY HIS LORDSHIP'S MOST OBEDIENT HUMBLE SERVANT JOHN CALEF, AGENT FOR THE INHABITANTS OF THE DISTRICT OF PENOBSCOT. SAMUEL JNO. NEELE SCULPT.

[London, 1781]
39 x 47 cm.
In John Calef, *The Siege of Penobscot by the Rebels* (London: G. Kearsley, 1781).
Scale ca. 1:9,500.
Oriented with north toward the upper right.
Relief shown by hachures; soundings in fathoms.
Includes "explanation" A–I, K–U, W–Z, a.
Inset: "Chart of Penobscot River" (see map 39a).

Reference. Reproduced in *Atlas of the American Revolution,* no. 36 (main map only).

Copy described. ICN.

Military information. Large, detailed plan. Locates the ships at various stages of the engagement and gives specifics as to land positions, fortifications, artillery, and strength of the forces on both sides, keyed to the "explanation." There are considerable differences in the configuration of the shoreline between this and the inset map.

39a

CHART OF PENOBSCOT RIVER
    [London, 1781]
    20 x 47 cm.
    Inset on map 39.
    Scale ca. 1:44,330.
    Oriented with north toward the right.
    Soundings in fathoms.
    Includes "explanation" A–I, K–X.

Military information. Shows the fort with relation to the river up which the American ships sailed and were captured or destroyed. All of the ships are depicted; many of them are named.

40

ATTACK OF THE REBELS UPON FORT PENOBSCOT IN THE PROVINCE OF NEW ENGLAND IN WHICH THEIR FLEET WAS TOTALLY DESTROYED AND THEIR ARMY DISPERSED THE 14TH AUGST. 1779. BY AN OFFICER PRESENT. FOR THE CONTINUATION (AFTER TINDAL'S) OF RAPIN'S HISTORY OF ENGD.
    [London], Decr. 18th 1785.
    36 x 39 cm.
    From Paul de Rapin-Thoyras, *Rapin's Impartial History of England . . . with the Continuation to the Year 1786,* 5 vols. (London: J. Harrison, 1784–89).
    Scale ca. 1:14,700.
    Relief shown by hachures.
    Includes a thirteen-line note on the battle.
    Although presumably issued with the volume cited above, all copies examined have been separates.

Reference. Reproduced in *American Heritage Book of the Revolution,* p. 290.

Copy described. MiU-C.

Military information. Shows positions of many ships (English ships are named and the number of cannon indicated) and fort and shore batteries.

2
QUEBEC TO ALBANY THEATER

INVASION OF CANADA   AUGUST 1775–OCTOBER 1776
Arnold's March   13 September–9 November 1775

41

A GENERAL MAP OF THE NORTHERN BRITISH COLONIES IN AMERICA, WHICH COMPREHENDS THE PROVINCE OF QUEBEC, THE GOVERNMENT OF NEWFOUNDLAND, NOVA-SCOTIA, NEW-ENGLAND AND NEW-YORK. FROM THE MAPS PUBLISHED BY THE ADMIRALTY AND BOARD OF TRADE, REGULATED BY THE ASTRONOMIC AND TRIGONOMETRIC OBSERVATIONS OF MAJOR HOLLAND, AND CORRECTED FROM GOVERNOR POWNALL'S LATE MAP 1776
London: Robt. Sayer & Jno. Bennett, 14th August 1776.
49 x 67 cm.
In Robert Sayer and John Bennett, *The American Military Pocket Atlas* (London, [1776]), no. 3.
Scale ca. 1:3,750,000.
Title in upper margin: "The Seat of War in the Northern Colonies . . . ."
Relief shown pictorially.
Prime meridian: London.

Reference. Reproduced in *Atlas of the American Revolution,* pp. 12–13.

Copy described. ICN.

Military information. Shows the route of Benedict Arnold's march to Quebec in 1775.

42

A VIEW OF THE RIVERS KENEBEC AND CHAUDIERE, WITH COLONEL ARNOLD'S ROUTE TO QUEBEC. LOND. MAG.

[London]: R. Baldwin, Septr. 1776.

18 x 12 cm.

In *London Magazine* 45 (1776): opp. 480.

Scale ca. 1:2,325,000.

Reference. Reproduced in Guthorn, *British Maps*, p. 68.

Copy described. ICHi.

Military information. A simple map showing only the rivers and portages used by Arnold. His route is shown as a dotted line.

43

A MAP OF THE INHABITED PART OF CANADA, FROM THE FRENCH SURVEYS, WITH THE FRONTIERS OF NEW YORK AND NEW ENGLAND FROM THE LARGE SURVEY BY CLAUDE JOSEPH SAUTHIER. ENGRAVED BY WM. FADEN, 1777
London: Wm. Faden, Feby. 25, 1777.

57 x 86 cm.

In William Faden, *The North American Atlas* (London, 1777), no. 3.

Scale ca. 1:798,000.

Relief shown by hachures.

Variants. A later state contains a table entitled "Winter Quarters of the King's Army in Canada, 1776" and a dedication to General Burgoyne. A third state retains the dedication, but the table has been erased from the plate.

Copy described. MiU-C.

Military information. Shows the route of Benedict Arnold's march to Quebec in 1775.

Quebec City   31 December 1775–1 January 1776

44

PLAN OF THE CITY AND ENVIRONS OF QUEBEC, WITH ITS SIEGE AND BLOCKADE BY THE AMERICANS, FROM THE 8TH OF DECEMBER 1775 TO THE 13TH OF MAY 1776. ENGRAVED BY WM. FADEN
London: Wm. Faden, 12 Septemr. 1776.

45 x 62 cm.
Scale ca. 1:7,000.
Relief shown by hachures.
Includes "references" A–M.
Served as the source for a French map of 1777 (map 45).
Also published in Faden's *North American Atlas* (London, 1777), no. 4.

References. Reproduced separately by Historic Urban Plans; in *Atlas of the American Revolution*, no. 6.

Copy described. ICN.

Military information. Shows the American artillery positions, indicating number of guns, and the deployment of Arnold's troops on the Plains of Abraham. The fortifications of the city are delineated, and the "references" include the positions where Montgomery and Arnold began their attack on 31 December 1775. Lines of fire from the battery across the Saint Lawrence at Point Lévis are shown.

45

ENVIRONS DE QUEBEC: BLOQUE PAR LES AMERICAINS DU 8. DECEMBRE 1775 AU 13. MAI 1776
Paris: Le Rouge, 1777.
23 x 30 cm.
Scale ca. 1:72,000.
Includes references A–I, K–Y.
Reduced from Faden's plan of 12 September 1776 (map 44).

Copy described. DLC.

Military information. As on map 44.

Valcour Island, N. Y.   11 October 1776

46

A SURVEY OF LAKE CHAMPLAIN, INCLUDING LAKE GEORGE, CROWN POINT, AND ST. JOHN. SURVEYED BY ORDER OF HIS EXCELLENCY MAJOR-GENERAL SR. JEFFERY AMHERST, KNIGHT

OF THE MOST HONBLE. ORDER OF THE BATH, COMMANDER IN CHIEF OF HIS MAJESTY'S FORCES IN NORTH AMERICA, (NOW LORD AMHERST). BY WILLIAM BRASSIER, 1762

> London: Robt. Sayer & Jno. Bennett, Augst. 5th 1776 [i.e., not before November 1776].
> 67 x 50 cm.
> In Robert Sayer and John Bennett, *The American Military Pocket Atlas* (London, [1776]), no. 6.
> Scale ca. 1:400,000.
> Relief shown by hachures.
> Includes "explanation of the engagement between Valcour Island and the western shore, October the 11th 1776" A–I.
> Inset: "A Particular Plan of Lake George, Surveyed in 1756. By Capt. Jackson."
> Also published in Thomas Jefferys, *The American Atlas* (London: R. Sayer and J. Bennett, 1778), no. 18.

References. Stevens and Tree 25b. Reproduced in *Atlas of the American Revolution*, no. 9.

Variants. Stevens and Tree identify an earlier state, which does not show the Battle of Valcour Island, and a later state dated 12 May 1794.

Copy described. ICN.

Military information. The Battle of Valcour Island is depicted with tiny boats keyed to the "explanation."

47

THE ATTACK AND DEFEAT OF THE AMERICAN FLEET UNDER BENEDICT ARNOLD BY THE KINGS FLEET COMMANDED BY SIR GUY CARLETON, UPON LAKE CHAMPLAIN THE 11TH OF OCTOBER, 1776. FROM A SKETCH TAKEN BY AN OFFICER ON THE SPOT. ENGRAVED BY WM. FADEN

> London: Wm. Faden, Decr. 3d, 1776.
> 26 x 42 cm.
> Scale ca. 1:71,000.
> Relief shown by hachures.

Also published in Faden's *North American Atlas* (London, 1777), no. 15.

References. Stevens and Tree 24a. A later state (Stevens and Tree 24b) is reproduced in *Atlas of the American Revolution,* no. 10. Portion showing military information only reproduced in William L. Clements Library, University of Michigan, *British Maps,* front.; *American Heritage Book of the Revolution,* p. 132.

Variants. A later state, with "Sir Guy Carleton" in the title replaced by "Captn. Thos. Pringle," is identified as Stevens and Tree 24a*. A variant copy of that state, with a letterpress account of the battle printed below the map, is identified as 24b.

Copy described. KN.

Military information. Shows the positions of the fleets during the attack, and their courses to and from the action. Five British ships are named.

BURGOYNE'S EXPEDITION   JUNE–OCTOBER 1777

48

A MAP OF THE COUNTRY IN WHICH THE ARMY UNDER LT. GENERAL BURGOYNE ACTED IN THE CAMPAIGN OF 1777, SHEWING THE MARCHES OF THE ARMY & THE PLACES OF THE PRINCIPAL ACTIONS. DRAWN BY MR. MEDCALFE & ENGRAVED BY WM. FADEN

London: Wm. Faden, Feby. 1st 1780.

57 x 28 cm.

Scale ca. 1:633,000.

Relief shown by hachures.

Possibly derived from the manuscript "Map of Part of the Province of New-York, East of Lakes George and Champlain. Per Simon Metcalfe, Deputy Surveyor [1772]" listed in New York State Library, *Catalogue of Maps,* p. 180.

Variant. Variant copies, on thinner paper, appear in Burgoyne's *State of the Expedition.*

Copy described. ICN.

Military information. Shows Lakes George and Champlain and all but the northeast part of Vermont. Route of troops from Fort Ticonderoga to Stillwater is shown in red, individual battles marked by crossed swords.

49

VIEW OF THE WHOLE ARMY ENCAMPED IN LINE OF BATTLE
  [London, 1780]
  On sheet 20 x 27 cm.
  In John Burgoyne, *A Supplement to the State of the Expedition from Canada, Containing General Burgoyne's Orders* (London: J. Robson, 1780), p. 9.
  Not drawn to scale.
  Entire map printed from type and printer's rules.

Copy described. ICN.

Military information. This is a schematic map or diagram, showing locations of the various brigades and regiments with respect to one another.

Ticonderoga, N. Y.   2–5 July 1777

50

[MAP OF TICONDEROGA, MOUNT INDEPENDENCE AND THE ADJACENT COUNTRY]
  [Philadelphia, 1778]
  31 x 26 cm.
  In Arthur St. Clair, *Proceedings of a General Court Martial . . . for the Trial of Major General St. Clair* (Philadelphia: Hall and Sellers, 1778), opp. p. 52.
  Scale ca. 1:29,260.
  Title from page 28.
  Oriented with north toward the right.
  Relief shown by hachures.
  On p. 52: "Explanation of the draught annexed" A–I, K–V, X–Z, 2–9.

References. Wheat and Brun 328. Reproduced in *Atlas of the American Revolution*, no. 17.

Copy described. ICN.

Military information. Together with the "Explanation," this detailed plan shows how the British, after landing on the shore of Lake Champlain, were able to overrun the stronghold. It also indicates the various fortified defensive positions and details how many men would have been required to successfully defend the post. The roads, forests, hills, ravines, and military and naval positions are depicted.

Hubbardton, Vt.   7 July 1777

51

PLAN OF THE ACTION AT HUBERTON UNDER BRIGADIER GENL. FRAZER, SUPPORTED BY MAJOR GENL. REIDESEL, ON THE 7TH JULY 1777. DRAWN BY P. GERLACH DEPUTY QUARTER MASTER GENERAL. ENGRAVED BY WM. FADEN
London: W. Faden, Feby. 1st 1780.
28 x 36 cm.
Scale ca. 1:7,200.
Relief shown by hachures.
Includes "references" A–I, O.

Reference. Reproduced in *Atlas of the American Revolution,* no. 18.

Variant. Variant copies, on thinner paper, appear in Burgoyne's *State of the Expedition.*

Copy described. ICN.

Military information. A large-scale battle plan indicating positions of both sides before and after the engagement and the lines of movement of the individual units. Terrain features influencing the tactics are prominently displayed.

Bennington, Vt.   6–16 August 1777

52

POSITION OF THE DETACHMENT UNDER LIEUTT. COLL. BAUM AT WALMSCOCK NEAR BENNINGTON, SHEWING THE ATTACKS OF THE ENEMY ON THE 16TH AUGUST 1777. DRAWN BY LIEUTT. DURNFORD, ENGINEER. ENGRAVED BY WM. FADEN 1780

London: W. Faden, Feby. 1st 1780.
27 x 35 cm.
Scale ca. 1:7,200.
Orientation not indicated.
Relief shown by hachures.
Includes "references" A–G.

Reference. Reproduced in *Atlas of the American Revolution*, no. 19.

Variant. Variant copies, on thinner paper, appear in Burgoyne's *State of the Expedition.*

Copy described. ICN.

Military information. The high bluff that the Hessian dragoons tried to defend and their fortification, as well as the deployment of the encircling American units, are depicted.

Saratoga, N. Y.   First Battle   19 September 1777

53

PLAN OF THE ENCAMPMENT AND POSITION OF THE ARMY UNDER HIS EXCELLY. LT. GENERAL BURGOYNE AT SWORDS HOUSE ON HUDSON'S RIVER NEAR STILLWATER ON SEPTR. 17TH WITH THE POSITIONS OF THAT PART OF THE ARMY ENGAGED ON THE 19TH SEPTR. 1777. DRAWN BY W. C. WILKINSON, LT. 62D REGT. ASST. ENGR. ENGRAVED BY WM. FADEN
London: W. Faden, Feby. 1st 1780.
32 x 35 cm.
Scale ca. 1:14,700.
Overlay (11 x 15 cm.) tipped on in upper right corner shows "third and fourth positions of that part of the army engaged on the 19th of September."
Oriented with north to the bottom.
Relief shown by hachures.

Reference. Reproduced in *Atlas of the American Revolution*, no. 20.

Variant. Variant copies, on thinner paper, appear in Burgoyne's *State of the Expedition.*

Copy described. ICN.

Military information. Fine, detailed plan indicating ground cover as well as relief. Shows British forces by unit, their lines of march, and location of the American army.

Forts Clinton and Montgomery   6 October 1777

54

A PLAN OF FORT MONTGOMERY & FORT CLINTON, TAKEN BY HIS MAJESTY'S FORCES UNDER THE COMMAND OF MAJ. GENL. SIR HENRY CLINTON, K: B: SURVEY'D BY MAJOR HOLLAND
   [London]: J. F. W. Des Barres, 1st Jany. 1779.
   54 x 79 cm.
   In J. F. W. Des Barres, *The Atlantic Neptune,* 4 vols. (London, 1774–82) 4: no. 23.
   Scale varies, but ca. 1:9,400 between forts (not 1:6,000 as indicated by graphic scale).
   Relief shown by hachures and shading.
   Includes "references" a-i, k-o.
   Inset: "Part of Hudsons River, Shewing the Position of Fort Montgomery and Fort Clinton, with the *chevaux de frieze,* Cables, Chains, &c. to Obstruct the Passage of His Majesty's Forces up the River. By Lieutt. John Knight of the Royal Navy, in 1777."

References. Henry N. Stevens, "Catalogue," no. 156. Reproduced by Barre Publishers, no. 34.

Copy described. ICN.

Military information. Shows ships in river, chains across river, "trees cut down to obstruct the approach to the forts," etc. Despite its title, the inset shows only the location of the *chevaux de frieze.*

55

PLAN OF THE ATTACK OF THE FORTS CLINTON & MONTGOMERY UPON HUDSONS RIVER, WHICH WERE STORMED BY HIS MAJESTYS FORCES UNDER THE COMMAND OF SIR HENRY CLINTON, K. B. ON THE 6TH OF OCTR. 1777. DRAWN FROM THE SURVEYS

OF VERPLANK, HOLLAND & METCALFE, BY JOHN HILLS, LT. 23D
REGT. AND ASST. ENGINEER
  London: Wm. Faden, June 1st 1784.
  67 x 52 cm.
  Scale ca. 1:21,500.
  Relief shown by shading.

References. Stevens and Tree 21a. Reproduced in *Atlas of the American Revolution,* no. 21.

Variant. A later state (Stevens and Tree 21b) was published in Stedman's *History.*

Copy described. ICN.

Military information. The large scale and careful delineation of the mountains and steep valleys in the Hudson River highlands make this an effective map for interpreting these engagements. The landings, lines of march, and troop locations are shown with some units named. The defenses of the two forts are indicated in detail. Twenty ships are depicted on the river; some are named and the commanders indicated.

Saratoga, N. Y.   Second Battle   7 October 1777

56

PLAN OF THE ENCAMPMENT AND POSITION OF THE ARMY UNDER HIS EXCELLY. LT. GENERAL BURGOYNE AT BRAEMUS HEIGHTS ON HUDSON'S RIVER NEAR STILLWATER, ON THE 20TH SEPTR. WITH THE POSITION OF THE DETACHMENT &C. IN THE ACTION OF THE 7TH OF OCTR. & THE POSITION OF THE ARMY ON THE 8TH OCTR. 1777. DRAWN BY W. C. WILKINSON, LT. 62 REGT. ASST. ENGR. ENGRAVED BY WM. FADEN
  London: W. Faden, Feby. 1st 1780.
  34 x 36 cm.
  Scale ca. 1:14,700.
  Overlay (15 x 10 cm.) tipped on at lower left corner shows positions on October 8th.
  Oriented with north to the bottom.

Relief shown by hachures.

Reference. Reproduced in *Atlas of the American Revolution,* no. 22.

Variant. Variant copies, on thinner paper, appear in Burgoyne's *State of the Expedition.*

Copy described. ICN.

Military information. Similar in format and treatment to Wilkinson's map of the first Battle of Saratoga (map 53). Shows American units proceeding northward from strongly fortified positions, intercepting the British advanced units. All British units are identified by regiment.

Saratoga, N. Y. Surrender 17 October 1777

57

PLAN OF THE POSITION WHICH THE ARMY UNDER LT. GENL. BURGOINE TOOK AT SARATOGA ON THE 10TH OF SEPTEMBER 1777, AND IN WHICH IT REMAINED TILL THE CONVENTION WAS SIGNED. ENGRAVED BY WM. FADEN
[London]: Wm. Faden, Feby. 1st 1780.
22 x 48 cm.
Scale ca. 1:11,000.
Oriented with north to the right.
Relief shown by hachures.
Served as the source for a German map of 1795 (map 58).

Reference. Reproduced in *Atlas of the American Revolution,* no. 23.

Variants. Variant copies, on thinner paper, appear in Burgoyne's *State of the Expedition.* A later state appears in Stedman's *History.*

Copy described. ICN.

Military information. Locates individual units of British, Hessians, and Americans. Troops are identified by regiment or commander. Artillery is located as is the bridge of boats across the Hudson used earlier by the British.

58

PLAN VON DER STELLING WELCHE DIE ARMEE UNTER DEM GEN. LIEUT. BURGOYNE BEY SARATOGA AM 10TEN SEPT. 1777 NAHM, UND IN WELCHER SIE BIS ZUR UNTERZEICHNUNG DER CONVENTION BLIEB

[Berlin, 1795]

11 x 24 cm.

In Charles Stedman, *Geschichte des Ursprungs, des Fortgangs und der Beendigung des amerikanischen Kriegs,* 2 vols. (Berlin: In der Vossischen Buchhandlung, 1795), Bd. 1.

Scale ca. 1:22, 150.

Oriented with north to the right.

Relief shown by hachures.

Reduced from Faden's plan of 1 February 1780 (map 57).

Copy described. DLC.

Military information. As on map 57.

Travels of the Convention Army   after 19 October 1777

59

MAP FOR THE INTERIOR TRAVELS THROUGH AMERICA, DELINEATING THE MARCH OF THE ARMY. T. CONDER SCULPSIT

[London, 1789]

41 x 37 cm.

In [Thomas Anburey], *Travels Through the Interior Parts of America,* 2 vols. (London: William Lane, 1789) 1: front.

Scale ca. 1:2,520,000.

Relief shown pictorially.

Prime meridian: London.

Includes a six-line "explanation."

Copy described. ICN.

Military information. Shows by means of colored lines "the marches of the army during the campaign after taking Ticonderoga," "the march of the officers, when separated from the private soldiers at Lancaster, to New York," "the extent of parole to the German officers," etc.

3
THE WAR IN THE CAROLINAS AND GEORGIA

60

THE MARCHES OF LORD CORNWALLIS IN THE SOUTHERN PROVINCES, NOW STATES OF NORTH AMERICA, COMPREHENDING THE TWO CAROLINAS, WITH VIRGINIA AND MARYLAND, AND THE DELAWARE COUNTIES. BY WILLIAM FADEN
London: Wm. Faden, Augst. 3, 1785.
65 x 49 cm.
Scale ca. 1:1,525,000.
Relief shown pictorially.
Prime meridian: London.

Variant. A later state, with the imprint date changed to "Feby. 3, 1787" and with Tarleton's route added to the references, appears in Tarleton's *History.*

Copy described. ICN.

Military information. Locates courthouses and Indian towns. "References" are designed to show Cornwallis's route in red, O'Hara's in blue. This copy lacks blue coloring.

61

SOUTH-CAROLINA AND PARTS ADJACENT, SHEWING THE MOVEMENTS OF THE AMERICAN AND BRITISH ARMIES
[Trenton, 1785]
50 x 58 cm.
In David Ramsay, *History of the Revolution of South-Carolina,* 2 vols. (Trenton: Isaac Collins, 1785) 2: front.
Scale ca. 1:1,037,500.
Relief shown by hachures.
Prime meridian: London.

Includes six lines of "references."

Served as the source for a map in the French edition of Ramsay (map 62).

Reference. Wheat and Brun 597.

Copy described. ICN.

Military information. Shows American and British encampments and marches, locations of battles.

62

CAROLINE MERIDIONALE, AVEC LES PARTIES ADJACENTES: POUR SERVIR À L'INTELLIGENCE DES MOUVEMENS DES ARMÉES AMÉRICAINES ET BRITANNIQUES. PICQUET SCULPT.

[Paris, 1787]

37 x 42 cm.

In David Ramsay, *Histoire de la révolution d'Amerique,* 2 vols. (London and Paris, 1787) 2: opp. p. 1.

Scale ca. 1:1,368,000.

Relief shown by hachures.

Prime meridian: Charleston.

Includes seven lines of "renvois."

Reduced from a map in the Trenton, 1785 edition of Ramsay (map 61).

Copy described. ICN.

Military information. As on map 61.

63

THE CAROLINA'S WITH PART OF GEORGIA. ENGRAVED FOR DR. GORDON'S HISTORY OF THE AMERICAN WAR. T. CONDER SCULPT.

London, [1788]

35 x 37 cm.

In William Gordon, *History of the Rise, Progress, and Establishment of the Independence of the United States,* 4 vols. (London, 1788) 3: front.

Scale ca. 1:1,625,000.

Relief shown pictorially.

Prime meridian: London.

"Plate VI. To face the title of vol. III."

Copy described. ICN.

Military information. Shows routes of the various armies with battles indicated by crossed swords.

Sullivan's Island, S. C.   28 June 1776
See also entry: 86a

64

A PLAN OF THE ATTACK OF FORT SULIVAN, NEAR CHARLES TOWN IN SOUTH CAROLINA, BY A SQUADRON OF HIS MAJESTY'S SHIPS, ON THE 28TH OF JUNE 1776, WITH THE DISPOSITION OF THE KING'S LAND FORCES AND THE ENCAMPMENTS AND ENTRENCHMENTS OF THE REBELS. FROM THE DRAWINGS MADE ON THE SPOT. ENGRAVED BY WILLIAM FADEN
London: Wm. Faden, Augt. 10th 1776.
28 x 38 cm.
Scale ca. 1:26,200.
Soundings shown in feet.
Inset: "Plan of the Platform in Sulivans Fort, by Lt. Colonel Thos. James" (see map 64a).
Dedication (printed from a separate plate): "To Commodore Sir Peter Parker . . . by Lt. Colonel Thos. James . . ."
Served as the source for a French map of 1777 (map 67a).
A later state was published in Faden's *North American Atlas* (London, 1777), no. 29.

Reference. Reproduced in *Atlas of the American Revolution*, no. 8.

Variants. Stevens and Tree identify variant copies (14a-d) with a letterpress "list of His Majesty's Squadron" and an account of the attack printed below the map; other non-plate variations lack the dedication and/or are printed on different-sized sheets. They also identify two later states in which the defenses around Sullivan's Fort become more and more impregnable.

Copy described. DLC.

Military information. Sullivan's Fort, later to be called Fort

Moultrie, appears at the southwest end of the island with nine British ships depicted standing off shore firing on the fort. Positions of the defenders on the mainland and at the northeast end of the island are indicated. The island to the northeast where Clinton landed his army is shown with the encampment.

64a

PLAN OF THE PLATFORM IN SULIVANS FORT, BY LT. COLONEL THOS. JAMES
    [London, 10 August 1776]
    10 x 20 cm.
    Inset on map 64.
    Scale ca. 1:1,760.
    Served as the source for an inset on a French map of 1777 (map 67b).

Military information. Ground plan of the finished portion of the fort, showing location of cannon and mortar.

65

AN EXACT PLAN OF CHARLES-TOWN-BAR AND HARBOUR, FROM AN ACTUAL SURVEY. WITH THE ATTACK OF FORT SULIVAN, ON THE 28TH OF JUNE 1776, BY HIS MAJESTY'S SQUADRON, COMMANDED BY SIR PETER PARKER
    London: Robt. Sayer and Jno. Bennett, 31st August 1776.
    51 x 70 cm.
    Scale 1:31,680 or "half a mile to an inch."
    Oriented with north toward the right.
    Relief shown pictorially; soundings in feet and fathoms.
    Includes "references" A–I, K–L, and sailing directions.
    Also published in *The North American Pilot*, 2 vols. (London: Sayer and Bennett, 1778–79) 2: no. 8.
    Served as the source for a map published in Paris in 1778 (map 69).

Reference. Reproduced in *Atlas of the American Revolution*, no. 7.

Variant. A later state is known with an imprint date of "January 1st 1791."

Copy described. MiU-C.

Military information. Shows forts, locations of British and American fleets (some keyed to references), and troops.

66

A PLAN OF THE ATTACK OF FORT SULIVAN, THE KEY OF CHARLES TOWN, IN SOUTH CAROLINA, ON THE 28TH OF JUNE 1776, BY HIS MAJESTY'S SQUADRON COMMANDED BY SIR PETER PARKER. BY AN OFFICER ON THE SPOT
London: Robt. Sayer & Jno. Bennett, 7th Septr. 1776.
32 x 39 cm.
Scale ca. 1:20,700.
Oriented with north to the right.
Letterpress below map gives text of a letter from Parker to Mr. Stephens, Secy. of the Admiralty, dated "Within Charles-Town Bar, July 9th, 1776."
Served as the source for a map printed in Philadelphia in 1777 (map 68).

Copy described. DLC.

Military information. Locates British forces under Clinton on Long Island, American forces on mainland and north end of Sullivan's Island, Fort Sullivan, and flanking redoubts. Shows British squadron, naming the ships. Letterpress includes table of ships, listing name, number of guns, and commander.

67

AN ACCURATE MAP OF NORTH AND SOUTH CAROLINA WITH THEIR INDIAN FRONTIERS, SHEWING IN A DISTINCT MANNER ALL THE MOUNTAINS, RIVERS, SWAMPS, MARSHES, BAYS, CREEKS, HARBOURS, SANDBANKS AND SOUNDINGS ON THE COASTS; WITH THE ROADS AND INDIAN PATHS AS WELL AS THE BOUNDARY OR PROVINCIAL LINES, THE SEVERAL TOWNSHIPS AND OTHER DIVISIONS OF THE LAND IN BOTH THE PROVINCES. CARTE EXACTE DE LA CORALINE SEPTENTRIONALE ET MERIDIONALE AVEC LES FRONTIERES DES INDIENS. . . . FROM ACTUAL SURVEYS BY HENRY MOUZON AND OTHERS
Paris: Le Rouge, 1777.

99 x 143 cm.

In George Louis Le Rouge, *Atlas Ameriquain septentrional* (Paris, 1778), nos. 21 and 22.

Scale ca. 1:537,000.

Title at right middle of map: "Caroline septentrionale et meridionale, en 4 feuilles. Traduite de l'Anglois."

Relief shown by hachures.

Prime meridian: London.

Insets: "Attaques du Fort Sulivan" (see map 67a)— "Port de Port Royal"—"Barre et Port de Charlestown" —"Fort Sulivan" (see map 67b).

Derived directly from the map with the same title published by Sayer and Bennett, 30 May 1775.

References. Cumming no. 450; *Cartografia de Ultramar* 2: no. 46, with reproduction.

Copy described. DLC.

Military information. Limited to insets (see maps 67a and 67b).

67a

ATTAQUES DU FORT SULIVAN PRÈS CHARLESTOWN DANS LA CAROLINE MERIDIONALE PAR LES ANGLOIS LE 28 JUIN 1776 AVEC LES CAMPS DES AMERIQUAINS
[Paris, 1777]
33 x 24 cm.
Inset on map 67.
Scale ca. 1:30,000.
Oriented with north toward the upper left.
"Nota. Les chifres soulignées sont des brasses qui dépendent de la grande carte."
Reduced from Faden's map of 10 August 1776 (map 64).

Military information. As on map 64.

67b

FORT SULIVAN. PAR JAMES, LIEUTENANT COLONEL D'ARTILLERIE
[Paris, 1777]
8 x 19 cm.

Inset on map 67.

Scale ca. 1:1,760.

Derived from the inset on the Faden map of 10 August 1776 (map 64).

Military information. Ground plan of the finished portion of the fort.

68

A PLAN OF THE ATTACK OF FORT SULIVAN, THE KEY OF CHARLES TOWN IN SOUTH CAROLINA, ON THE 28TH OF JUNE 1776 BY HIS MAJESTY'S SQUADRON COMMANDED BY SIR PETER PARKER, BY AN OFFICER ON THE SPOT

Philadelphia: Printed for Daniel Humphreys by Styner and Cist [1777]

32 x 39 cm.

Scale ca. 1:21,120.

Oriented with north to the right.

Letterpress account below map begins "The following description of the attack of Fort Sulivan, was received in a letter from Sir Peter Parker to Mr. Stephens, Secretary of the Admiralty."

Derived directly from the Sayer and Bennett map with the same title (map 66). Apparently printed during the British occuption of Philadelphia.

Reference. Wheat and Brun 592.

Copy described. MiU-C.

Military information. As on map 66.

69

BARRE ET PORT DE CHARLES-FOWN [*sic*] LEVÉ EN 1776, AVEC LES ATTAQUES DU FORT SULWAN [*sic*] DU 28. JUIN 1776, PAR L'ESCADRE ANGLAISE COMMANDÉE PAR P. PARKER

Paris: Le Rouge, 1778.

45 x 62 cm.

Scale ca. 1:33,300.

Oriented with north toward the right.

Relief shown pictorially; soundings in feet and fathoms.

Reduced from the Sayer and Bennett map of 31 August 1776 (map 65).

Variants. A later state exists, greatly reworked, with the title moved and corrected, and with the addition of a note and an inset ("Entrée de Charles-Town par dessan cape. des vaissaux"). A further state adds a second note.

Copy described. KN.

Military information. As on map 65.

70

A PLAN OF CHARLES TOWN THE CAPITAL OF SOUTH CAROLINA, WITH THE HARBOUR, ISLANDS, AND FORTS; THE ATTACK ON FORT SULIVAN BY HIS MAJESTY'S SHIPS UNDER SIR PETER PARKER IN 1776; THE POSITION OF THE LAND FORCES UNDER GENERAL CLINTON, AND THE REBEL CAMP AND INTRENCHMENTS EXACTLY DELINEATED. JNO. LODGE SCULP.
[London, February 1780]
14 x 29 cm.
In *Political Magazine* 1 (1780): opp. 116.
Scale ca. 1:63,360.
Soundings in fathoms.

Reference. Reproduced in Winsor, *Narrative and Critical History*, 6:170.

Copy described. ICN.

Military information. Shows ships bombarding Fort Sullivan, ships in Cooper River, "rebel camp" and entrenchments. British first and second brigades located.

71

CHARLES TOWN, SOUTH CAROLINA, WITH A CHART OF THE BARS & HARBOUR. BY R. COWLEY. JNO. LODGE SCULP.
[London]: Fielding & Walker, 1st of June 1780.
19 x 19 cm.
Scale ca. 1:56,700.
Oriented with north to the right.
Soundings in fathoms.

Copy described. DLC.

Military information. Shows numerous forts, tiny depiction of "Actaeon" and "Sphinx," Clinton's advanced post (on mainland!). Has fort on bridge connecting Sullivan's Island with mainland.

72

A SKETCH OF THE SITUATION & STATIONS OF THE BRITISH VESSELS, UNDER THE COMMAND OF SIR PETER PARKER, ON THE ATTACK UPON FORT MOULTRIE ON SULIVAN ISLAND, JUNE 28TH 1776. ABERNETHIE SCULPT., CHARLESTON
>[Trenton, 1785]
>17 x 29 cm.
>In David Ramsay, *History of the Revolution of South-Carolina,* 2 vols. (Trenton: Isaac Collins, 1785) 1: opp. 144.
>Scale ca. 1:10,980.
>Oriented with north to the left.
>Served as the source for a map in the French edition of Ramsay (map 73) and another in Gordon's *History* (map 86a).

Reference. Wheat and Brun 596.

Copy described. ICN.

Military information. Shows and names nine British ships attacking the fort.

73

PLAN DE LA SITUATION ET DES STATIONS DES VAISSEAUX BRITAN-NIQUES, SOUS LE COMMANDEMENT DE SIR PIERRE PARKER, À L'ATTAQUE DU FORT MOULTRIE, DANS L'ISLE SULLIVAN, LE 28. JUIN 1776. PICQUET SCULP.
>[Paris, 1787]
>16 x 29 cm.
>In David Ramsay, *Histoire de la révolution d' Amérique,* 2 vols. (London and Paris, 1787) 1: opp. 126.
>Scale ca. 1:10,980.

Oriented with north to the left.

Relief shown by hachures.

Derived directly from a map in the Trenton, 1785 edition of Ramsay (map 72).

Copy described. ICN.

Military information. As on map 72.

Savannah, Ga.   29 December 1778

74

SKETCH OF THE NORTHERN FRONTIERS OF GEORGIA, EXTENDING FROM THE MOUTH OF THE RIVER SAVANNAH TO THE TOWN OF AUGUSTA. BY ARCHIBALD CAMPBELL. ENGRAVED BY WILLM. FADEN

London: Wm. Faden, May 1st 1780.

60 x 70 cm.

Scale ca. 1:111,500.

Oriented with north toward the upper right.

Inset: "Continuation of Savanna River, from Ebenezer to Augusta."

Includes "references to the Attack of Savannah on the 28th December 1778" 1–12.

References. Cf. Stevens and Tree 22a (an incorrect entry). Reproduced in Georgia Historical Society, *Collections* 8 (1913): opp. 32.

Variant. Stevens and Tree identify a variant copy (22b) on paper dated 1794.

Copy described. DLC.

Military information. Shows lines of British and rebels outside of Savannah and ships in river keyed to the "references."

Savannah, Ga.   9 October 1779

75

[A CHART OF THE COAST OF GEORGIA]
[London, 1780]
76 x 60 cm.

In J. F. W. Des Barres, *The Atlantic Neptune,* 4 vols. (London, 1774–82) 3:56.

Scale ca. 1:403,000.

Relief shown by shading.

Inset: "Plan of the Siege of Savannah" (map 75a).

Reference. Henry N. Stevens, "Catalogue," no. 168c.

Variants. Henry N. Stevens, "Catalogue," identifies two earlier states, both lacking the inset.

Copy described. DLC.

Military information. Limited to inset (see map 75a).

75a

PLAN OF THE SIEGE OF SAVANNAH, AND THE DEFEAT OF THE FRENCH AND REBELS ON 9TH OCTR. 1779 BY HIS MAJESTY'S FORCES UNDER THE COMMAND OF MAJOR GENERAL AUGUSTIN PREVOST. SURVEYED BY JOHN WILSON A[SST]. ENGINEER
[London, 1780]
21 x 32 cm.
Inset on map 75.
Scale ca. 1:17,420.
Oriented with north toward the upper right.
Relief shown by shading.

Military information. British defenses of city delineated in detail, keyed by number to separate explanation sheet. The "Rebel camp" and French encampments are indicated as are lines of march and approaches for the siege.

76

PLAN OF THE SIEGE OF SAVANNAH, WITH THE JOINT ATTACK OF THE FRENCH AND AMERICANS ON THE 9TH OCTOBER 1779, IN WHICH THEY WERE DEFEATED BY HIS MAJESTY'S FORCES UNDER THE COMMAND OF MAJOR GENL. AUGUSTIN PREVOST. FROM A SURVEY BY AN OFFICER
London: Printed for Wm. Faden, Feby. 2d 1784.
42 x 58 cm.
Scale ca. 1:4,500.

Oriented with north toward the bottom.
Relief shown by hachures.
Includes "references" 1–14, A–I, and a note.

References. Reproduced separately by Historic Urban Plans (2d state); in *Atlas of the American Revolution*, no. 39.

Variant. A later state appears in Stedman's *History.*

Copy described. ICN.

Military information. Shows fortifications, gun emplacements, troop locations. All British and loyalist troops are named in the references. "Total number fit for duty" given as 2,360.

Charleston Expedition   19 March–12 May 1780

77

A PLAN OF THE MILITARY OPERATIONS AGAINST CHARLESTOWN. THE ARMY BEING COMMANDED BY L. G. SIR HENRY CLINTON, K. B. AND THE FLEET BY VICE-ADMIRAL ARBUTHNOT, FROM AN ORIGINAL DRAWING SENT BY AN OFFICER IN THE ARMY
London: Robt. Sayer and John Bennett, 27 of May 1780.
44 x 54 cm.
Scale ca. 1:17,500.
Includes "references" A–I, K–M, a-i.

Reference. Reproduced in *Atlas of the Amercan Revolution*, no. 40.

Copy described. MiU-C.

Military information. Shows troop movements from landing at Edisto Inlet to siege of Charleston. Actions at Stono Creek and Stono Ferry and fleet locations indicated.

78

A PLAN OF THE TOWN, BAR, HARBOUR AND ENVIRONS OF CHARLESTOWN IN SOUTH CAROLINA, WITH ALL THE CHANNELS, SOUNDINGS, SAILING-MARKS &C. FROM THE SURVEYS MADE IN THE COLONY. ENGRAVED BY WILLIAM FADEN . . .1780

London: Wm. Faden, June 1st 1780.

50 x 68 cm.

Scale ca. 1:46,500.

Soundings in fathoms.

Copy described. RPJCB.

Military information. Limited to forts and location of barracks.

79

A SKETCH OF THE ENVIRONS OF CHARLESTOWN IN SOUTH CAROLINA. BY CAPT. GEORGE SPROULE, ASSISTANT ENGINEER, ON THE SPOT

[London], 1st June 1780.

41 x 55 cm.

From J. F. W. Des Barres, *The Atlantic Neptune,* 4 vols. (London, 1774–82).

Scale ca. 1:130,000.

Soundings in fathoms.

Includes references A–G, a-f.

References. Henry N. Stevens, "Catalogue," no. 163; Stevens and Tree 13a.

Variant. A later state exists (Stevens and Tree 13b) with the imprint date erased and numerous other changes.

Copy described. MiU-C.

Military information. Shows positions of British troops before the siege, with units identified by commander. The later state shows British forces above Charleston and the three parallels of the siege.

80

A SKETCH OF THE OPERATIONS BEFORE CHARLESTOWN THE CAPITAL OF SOUTH CAROLINA

[London]: I. F. W. Des Barres, 17 of June 1780.

104 x 77 cm.

In J. F. W. Des Barres, *The Atlantic Neptune,* 4 vols. (London, 1774–82).

Scale ca. 1:12,000.

Soundings in fathoms.

Inset: [Charlestown Harbour] (map 80a).

Includes references A–I, K–U, a-f; A–I, K–P; a-i, k-q.

Reference. Henry N. Stevens, "Catalogue," no. 164.

Variant. Henry N. Stevens, "Catalogue," refers to variant copies in which the imprint has been erased from the paper.

Copy described. ICN.

Military information. The most useful single plan for interpreting this campaign. The very large scale enables depiction of the military information pertaining to Clinton's successful siege of Charleston in great detail. The British forces are shown by regiment, keyed to the lengthy descriptive references. The parallels of the investment and defensive lines are clearly shown. British troops are colored red, Americans yellow. The ships of both fleets are illustrated; the legend names them and indicates number of guns for each.

80a

[CHARLESTOWN HARBOUR]
   [London, 17 June 1780]
   19 x 33 cm.
   Inset on map 80.
   Scale ca. 1:44,000.
   Relief shown by shading.
   Four lettered references are keyed to the legend on the main map.

Military information. Coverage is extended east of the area shown on the main map to include Sullivan's Island and the redoubts and batteries on Mount Pleasant. The fort, batteries, lines, bridge of boats, and several ships are shown.

81

A SKETCH OF CHARLESTON HARBOUR SHEWING THE DISPO-

SITION OF THE BRITISH FLEET UNDER THE COMMAND OF VICE ADML. MARIOT ARBUTHNOT UPON THE ATTACK ON FORT MOUL-TRIE ON SULIVAN ISLAND IN 1780. ABERNETHIE SCULPT., CHARLESTON

[Trenton, 1785]

17 x 30 cm.

In David Ramsay, *History of the Revolution of South-Carolina,* 2 vols. (Trenton: Isaac Collins, 1785) 2: opp. p. 52.

Scale ca. 1:50,000.

Relief shown by hachures.

Served as the source for a map in the French edition of Ramsay (map 85).

Reference. Wheat and Brun 593.

Copy described. ICN.

Military information. Shows fortifications around Charleston Harbor, ships, bridge of boats, etc.

82

A SKETCH OF THE OPERATIONS BEFORE CHARLESTON THE CAPITAL OF SOUTH CAROLINA, 1780. ABERNETHIE SCULPT.

[Trenton, 1785]

36 x 29 cm.

In David Ramsay, *History of the Revolution of South-Carolina,* 2 vols. (Trenton: Isaac Collins, 1785) 2: opp. 58.

Scale ca. 1:12,700.

Relief shown by hachures.

Includes references to "fortifications, outworks &c. under the command of Lt. General Lincoln" A–I, K–Q and "redoubts, approaches & batteries of the British army" 1–6, o-r.

Served as the source for a map in the French edition of Ramsay (map 84) and another in Gordon's *History* (map 86).

Reference. Wheat and Brun 594.

Variant. A later state (Wheat and Brun 595) changes the spelling "approatches" to "approaches."

Copy described. MiU-C.

Military information. Detailed engraving showing terrain features, defenses of the city, the chained line of boats across the Cooper River, the name and number of guns of ten American ships above the chain, and the three lines of approaches taken up by Clinton's forces during the siege.

83

PLAN OF THE SIEGE OF CHARLESTOWN IN SOUTH CAROLINA
London, March 1st 1787.
26 x 30 cm.
In Banastre Tarleton, *History of the Campaigns of 1780 and 1781* (London: T. Cadell, 1787), opp. p. 32.
Scale ca. 1:41,000.
Oriented with north toward the upper left.
Relief shown by hachures.
Served as the source for a map appearing in Stedman's *History* (map 87).

Copy described. ICN.

Military information. Shows the route of the British from the Stono to the Ashley River, the deployment of units on the Charleston Peninsula north of the city, the defensive fortification, and the three parallels of the siege. The British fleet is depicted in the harbor as is Fort Moultrie on Sullivan's Island, the bridge of boats to the mainland, and the boom erected between the town and Shute's Folly.

84

ESQUISSE DES OPÉRATIONS DU SIÉGE DE CHARLESTON, CAPITALE
DE LA CAROLINE MERIDIONALE, EN 1780. PICQUET SCULP.
[Paris, 1787]
36 x 29 cm.
In David Ramsay, *Histoire de la révolution d'Amérique*, 2 vols. (London and Paris, 1787) 2: opp. p. 70.
Scale ca. 1:12,700.

Relief shown by hachures.
Includes references to "fortifications, ouvrages exterieurs
&c sous le commandement du Lieutt. General Lincoln"
A–I, K–Q and "redoutes, approches et batteries de
l'armee Britannique" 1–6, o-r.
Derived directly from a map in the Trenton, 1785 edition
of Ramsay (map 82).

Copy described. ICN.

Military information. As on map 82.

85

PLAN DU HAVRE DE CHARLESTON, MONTRANT LA DISPOSITION DE
LA FLOTTE BRITANNIQUE, COMMANDÉE PAR LE VICE-AMIRAL
MARIE ARBUTHNOT, À L'ATTAQUE DU FORT MOULTRIE DANS
L'ISLE SULLIVAN, EN 1780. PICQUET SCULP.
[Paris, 1787]
17 x 30 cm.
In David Ramsay, *Histoire de la révolution d'Amérique*,
2 vols. (London and Paris, 1787) 2: opp. p. 62.
Scale ca. 1:51,480.
Relief shown by hachures.
Derived directly from a map in the Trenton, 1785 edition
of Ramsay (map 81).

Copy described. ICN.

Military information. As on map 81.

86

A SKETCH OF THE OPERATIONS BEFORE CHARLESTOWN, SOUTH
CAROLINA, 1780. ENGRAVED FOR DR. GORDON'S HISTORY OF THE
AMERICAN WAR. T.CONDER SCULPT.
[London, 1788]
29 x 17 cm.
In William Gordon, *History of the Rise, Progress, and
Establishment of the Independence of the United
States,* 4 vols. (London, 1788) 3: opp. p. 359.
Scale ca. 1:21,250.
Relief shown by hachures.

Includes references to "American fortifications &c." A–I, K–Q and "British approaches" 1–6, o-r.

Inset: "A Sketch of Sr. Peter Parker's Attack on Fort Moultrie June 28th 1776" (see map 86a).

"Plate VII. To face page 358 vol. III."

Reduced from a map in Ramsay's *History* (map 82).

Reference. Reproduced in *American Heritage* 9, no. 2 (February 1958):51.

Copy described. ICN.

Military information. As on map 82.

86a

A SKETCH OF SR. PETER PARKER'S ATTACK ON FORT MOULTRIE JUNE 28TH 1776

[London, 1788]

9 x 17 cm.

Inset on map 86.

Scale ca. 1:20,000.

Oriented with north to the left.

Relief shown by hachures.

Reduced from the map in Ramsay's *History* (map 72).

Reference. Reproduced in *American Heritage Book of the Revolution*, p. 134.

Copy described. ICN.

Military information. As on map 72.

87

PLAN OF THE SIEGE OF CHARLESTOWN IN SOUTH CAROLINA. ENGRAVED FOR STEDMANS HISTORY OF THE AMERICAN WAR

[London, 1794]

26 x 30 cm.

From Charles Stedman, *History of the Origin, Progress, and Termination of the American War*, 2 vols. (London: J. Murray, 1794) 2: opp. 185.

Scale ca. 1:41,000.

Oriented with north toward the upper left.

Relief shown by hachures.

Derived directly from the plan appearing in Tarleton's *History* (map 83).

Copy described. ICN.

Military information. As on map 83.

Camden, S. C. 16 August 1780

88

A NEW AND ACCURATE MAP OF NORTH CAROLINA AND PART OF SOUTH CAROLINA, WITH THE FIELD OF BATTLE BETWEEN EARL CORNWALLIS AND GENERAL GATES. JNO. LODGE SCULP.

London: J. Bew, Novr. 30th 1780.

28 x 40 cm.

In *Political Magazine* 1 (1780): opp. 739.

Scale ca. 1:1,300,000.

Relief shown pictorially.

Copy described. ICN.

Military information. Very limited—the engagement is indicated by two groups of tiny square symbols facing each other. Useful, however, in showing the roads and the strategic location of Camden in relation to the North and South Carolina theater.

89

A SKETCH OF THE BATTLE NEAR CAMDEN IN SOUTH CAROLINA, 16 AUGST. 1780

[London, 1780?]

30 x 32 cm.

In J. F. W. Des Barres, *The Atlantic Neptune*, 4 vols. (London, 1774–82) 3: no. 54.

Scale ca. 1:4,845.

Relief shown by shading.

Reference. Henry N. Stevens, "Catalogue," no. 165.

Copy described. DLC.

Military information. Very detailed locations of the opposing units shown by two-color rectangles. Each British unit is named, as are all the commanders for both sides. While the order of battle appears correct, the terrain (which differs considerably from the Faden plan in Tarleton) appears to be inaccurately delineated. In particular, Saunders Creek and ravine are not shown.

90

PLAN OF THE BATTLE FOUGHT NEAR CAMDEN, AUGUST 16TH 1780.

> London, March 1st 1787.
> 22 x 19 cm.
> In Banastre Tarleton, *History of the Campaigns of 1780 and 1781* (London: T. Cadell, 1787), opp. p. 108.
> Scale ca. 1:42,000.
> Oriented with north toward the upper right.
> Relief shown by hachures.
> Includes "references" 1–9.

Reference. Reproduced in *Atlas of the American Revolution,* no. 41.

Variant. A later state appears in Stedman's *History.*

Copy described. ICN.

Military information. The terrain is shown in sufficient detail to help interpret the action. The British line of march northward to the first order of battle is shown, as is the deployment of both armies by unit. The "references" name the British regiments, and the "flight of the Americans" and British pursuit are indicated.

Cowan's Ford, N. C.   1 February 1781

91

SKETCH OF THE CATAWBA RIVER AT MC COWANS FORD. ENGRAVED FOR STEDMANS HISTORY OF THE AMERICAN WAR

> [London], Feby. 6th 1794.
> 17 x 18 cm.
> In Charles Stedman, *History of the Origin, Progress, and Termination of the American War,* 2 vols. (London: J. Murray, 1794) 2: opp. 329.

Scale ca. 1:6,800.
Relief shown by hachures.

Copy described. ICN.

Military information. The only published plan of this engagement. The stretch of the Catawba River involved, and its islands, is shown. The lines of march of the British and their crossing, and the deployment of British and American forces on the east shore, are delineated.

Guilford Courthouse, N. C.   15 March 1781

92

BATTLE OF GUILDFORD, FOUGHT ON THE 15TH OF MARCH 1781
London; March 1st 1787.
22 x 19 cm.
In Banastre Tarleton, *History of the Campaigns of 1780 and 1781* (London: T. Cadell, 1787), opp. p. 276.
Scale ca. 1:18,800.
Oriented with north toward the upper left.
Relief shown by hachures.
Includes one reference, A.

Reference. Reproduced in *Atlas of the American Revolution*, no. 42.

Variant. A later state appears in Stedman's *History.*

Copy described. ICN.

Military information. British forces are indicated by rectangles for each unit, their initial order of battle colored red, their second and third positions in pink. The American forces are shown in several stages by unit with rectangles colored yellow. The lines of march are indicated.

Hobkirk's Hill, S. C.   25 April 1781

93

SKETCH OF THE BATTLE OF HOBKIRKS HILL, NEAR CAMDEN, ON THE 25TH APRIL 1781. DRAWN BY C. VALLANCEY, CAPTN. OF THE VOLS. OF IRELAND

[London]: Engraved and published by Wm. Faden, Augt. 1st 1783.

44 x 30 cm.

Scale not indicated.

Relief shown by hachures.

Reference. Reproduced in *Atlas of the American Revolution,* no. 43.

Variant. A later state appears in Stedman's *History.*

Copy described. ICN.

Military information. North of the destroyed "log town" the British deployment just before the drawn battle is indicated by diagonally shaded rectangles, the specific units are named, and the line of march northward to this point is indicated; also shown in considerable detail are General Greene's Virginia and Pennsylvania lines and militia.

4

THE WAR IN THE
MIDDLE COLONIES

94

CARTE DU THEATRE DE LA GUERRE DANS L'AMÉRIQUE SEPTEN-
TRIONALE, PENDANT LES ANNÉES 1775, 76, 77, ET 78 OÙ SE
TROUVENT LES PRINCIPAUX CAMPS AVEC LES DIFFERÉNTES PLACES
ET EPOQUES DES BATTAILLES QUI SE SONT DONNÉES PENDANT CES
CAMPAGNES. GRAVÉE D'APRÈS LE DESSEIN ORIGINAL QUI A ÉTÉ
PRÉSENTE AU ROI, FAIT PAR LE SR. CAPITAINE DU CHESNOY
　Paris: Perrier graveur [1779]
　66 x 75 cm.
　Scale ca. 1:1,016,000.
　Relief shown pictorially.

Copy described. RPJCB.

Military information. Shows position of Washington's army
at White Plains, encampments north of Philadelphia, and the
winter camp at Valley Forge. Battles from Lake Champlain
to Boston to Brandywine are indicated by crossed swords
with dates.

95

POSITION DER KOENIGL. GROSBRITTANISCHEN UND DERER VER-
EINIGTEN PROVINZIAL ARMEÉ IN NEW YORK UND DEM JERSEYS
IN NORD AMERICA IM JAHR 1780
　[Nuremberg: Homann Heirs, 1780?]
　35 x 44 cm.
　Scale ca. 1:1,076,000.
　Includes references in German and French a-i, k-p.

Copy described. MiU-C.

Military information. Although there were no major engagements in this theater in 1780, this map shows the encampments of the northern armies.

NEW YORK CAMPAIGN   JULY–NOVEMBER 1776

96

A VIEW OF THE PRESENT SEAT OF WAR, AT AND NEAR NEW-YORK
> [Boston, 1776]
> 13 x 9 cm.
> In Nathaniel Low, *An Astronomical Diary; or, Almanack
> . . . 1777* (Boston: J. Gill, [1776]).
> Scale ca. 1:507,000.
> Relief shown by hachures.
> Includes references A–I.

References. Wheat and Brun 386. Reproduced in Winsor, *Narrative and Critical History* 6: 342.

Copy described. MiU-C.

Military information. Primitive woodcut map, showing forts and "Gen. Washington's lines on New-York Island."

97

A VIEW OF THE PRESENT SEAT OF WAR AT AND NEAR NEW YORK
> [Hartford, Conn., 1776]
> 12 x 9 cm.
> In [Nathan Daboll], *Freebetter's New-England Almanack,
> for . . . 1777* (Hartford: N. Patten, [1776]).
> Scale ca. 1:507,000.
> Relief shown by hachures.
> Includes (on following page) "directions for the plate"
> A–I.

Reference. Wheat and Brun 385.

Copy described. MWA.

Military information. Primitive woodcut map, showing forts and "General Washington's lines on New-York Island."

98

[THE PRESENT SEAT OF WAR AT AND NEAR NEW YORK]
[Worcester, Mass., 1776]
12 x 9 cm.
In Samuel Stearns, *The North American's Almanack, for
. . . 1777* (Worcester: Stearns and Bigelow [1776]).
Scale ca. 1:507,000.
Relief shown by hachures.
Includes references A–I, K–L, N (references G, K–L, N
are on another page).

Reference. Wheat and Brun 383.

Variant. Wheat and Brun record a later state in which some
of the inserted type has been changed.

Copy described. MWA.

Military information. Primitive woodcut map, showing
"lines of the Continental Army on the east side of North-
River" and "the lines which guard the passage from the
Sound to Kings-Bridge."

99

A SKETCH OF THE OPERATIONS OF HIS MAJESTY'S FLEET AND
ARMY UNDER THE COMMAND OF VICE ADMIRAL THE RT. HBLE.
LORD VISCOUNT HOWE AND GENL. SR. WM. HOWE, K. B. IN
1776
[London]: J. F. W. Des Barres, Jany. 17, 1777.
82 x 60 cm. plus extra references on attached sheet 84 x
60 cm.
In J. F. W. Des Barres, *The Atlantic Neptune*, 4 vols. (Lon-
don, 1774–82) 4: no. 20.
Scale ca. 1:128,700.
Relief shown by hachures and shading; soundings in
fathoms.
Includes "references" A–I, K–Q and, on attached sheet,
"references" a-i, k-z; *a-i, k-y.*
Bottom half of attached sheet contains view: "The Phoe-

nix and the Rose Engaged by the Enemy's Fire Ships and Galleys on the 16 Augst. 1776."

References. Henry N. Stevens, "Catalogue," nos. 149, 150. Reproduced by Barre Publishers, no. 32.

Copy described. ICN.

Military information. One of the greatest of The *Atlantic Neptune* charts, with the best topographical information on the lower Hudson River valley, western Long Island, and Staten Island. Locates entrenchments, encampments, troop positions, etc. Some regiments are named. The map is accompanied, on the same double-folded sheet, by five aquatint shore profiles and the famous engraving of the engagement of the *Phoenix* and the *Rose,* after the painting by Dominick Serres.

100

MAP OF THE PROGRESS OF HIS MAJESTY'S ARMIES IN NEW YORK, DURING THE LATE CAMPAIGN, ILLUSTRATING THE ACCOUNTS PUBLISH'D IN THE LONDON GAZETTE
[London, January 1777]
20 x 32 cm.
In *Gentleman's Magazine* 46 (1776, Supplement): opp. 607.
Scale ca. 1:318,000.
Relief shown pictorially.

Reference. Reproduced, in part, in Winsor, *Narrative and Critical History* 6:404.

Copy described. ICN.

Military information. Shows "progress of the Kings troops," "retreat of the rebels," "English camp," "position of the two armies Oct. 25," etc.

101

A PLAN OF THE OPERATIONS OF THE KING'S ARMY UNDER THE COMMAND OF GENERAL SR. WILLIAM HOWE, K. B. IN NEW YORK AND EAST NEW JERSEY, AGAINST THE AMERICAN FORCES

COMMANDED BY GENERAL WASHINGTON, FROM THE 12TH OF OCTOBER TO THE 28TH OF NOVEMBER 1776. WHEREIN IS PARTICULARLY DISTINGUISHED THE ENGAGEMENT ON THE WHITE PLAINS, THE 28TH OF OCTOBER. BY CLAUDE JOSEPH SAUTHIER. ENGRAVED BY WM. FADEN, 1777
[London]: W. Faden, Feby. 25th 1777.
73 x 49 cm.
Scale ca. 1:88,000.
Relief shown by hachures.
Includes three lettered references A–B, A, plus numerous small notes.
Served as the source for a German map of the same year (map 102) and another of 1795 (map 106).
Also published in Faden's *North American Atlas* (London, 1777), no. 16.

References. Stevens and Tree 45a. Reproduced in *Atlas of the American Revolution,* no. 13.

Variants. Two later states are known. The first (Stevens and Tree 45b) adds British ships in the river off Tarrytown. The second appears in Stedman's *History.*

Copy described. DLC.

Military information. Shows in detail movements and encampments of the British and American units from the north shore of Long Island north to the Croton River, south to Fort Washington on upper Manhattan, and west to Fort Lee, New Jersey. Also the routes of the armies west and south of Fort Lee. Many engraved notations dscribe maneuvers and engagements.

102

PLAN VON DEN OPERATIONEN DER KOENIGLICHEN ARMEE UNTER DEM GENERAL SIR WILLIAM HOWE IN NEUYORCK UND OST-NEUJERSEŸ GEGEN DIE AMERICANER UNTER COMANDO DES GENERAL WASHINGTON, VOM 12. OCTOBER BIS 28. NOVEMBER 1776, WOBEŸ VORZÜGLICH DIE AFFAIRE BEŸ WHITE PLAINS AM 28. OCTOBER VORGESTELLT WIRD
[Nuremberg, 1777]

38 x 27 cm.

In [Christoph Heinrich Korn], *Geschichte der Kriege in und ausser Europa*, 30 pts. ([Nuremberg]: Gabriel N. Raspe, 1777–84) 5: pl. 1.

Scale ca. 1:162,200.

Relief shown by hachures.

Reduced from the Sauthier-Faden map (map 101).

Copy described. MiU-C.

Military information. As on map 101.

103

Campaign of MDCCLXXVI
   [London, 1780]
   53 x 45 cm.
   In [John Hall], *The History of the Civil War in America* (London: T. Payne, 1780), front.
   Scale ca. 1:220,000.
   Includes "explanation" A–I, K–R.
   Inset: "Campaign of MDCCLXXVII" (see map 103a).

Reference. Reproduced, in part, in Winsor, *Narrative and Critical History* 6:344.

Copy described. MiU-C.

Military information. Outline map featuring roads, sites of battles, and locations of military units. Covers battle of Long Island through White Plains to Fort Lee.

103a

Campaign of MDCCLXXVII
   [London, 1780]
   25 x 22 cm.
   Inset on map 103.
   Scale ca. 1:496,000.

Reference. Reproduced in Winsor, *Narrative and Critical History* 6:414.

Military information. Shows troop locations and battle sites for the encampments from Howe's landing at Head of Elk through the Battle of Germantown.

104

CHART AND PLAN OF THE HARBOUR OF NEW YORK & THE COUNY. ADJACENT, FROM SANDY HOOK TO KINGSBRIDGE, COM-PREHENDING THE WHOLE OF NEW YORK AND STATEN ISLANDS, AND PART OF LONG ISLAND & THE JERSEY SHORE: AND SHEW-ING THE DEFENCES OF NEW YORK BOTH BY LAND AND SEA. JNO. LODGE SCULP.
London: J. Bew, Novr. 30th 1781.
42 x 25 cm.
In *Political Magazine* 2 (1781): opp. 656.
Scale ca. 1:150,000.
Relief shown by hachures; soundings in fathoms.

Reference. Reproduced, in part, in Winsor, *Narrative and Critical History* 6: 343.

Copy described. ICN.

Military information. Several notes on Long Island indicate positions at various times between 1776 and 1778.

105

NEW YORK ISLAND & PARTS ADJACENT. ENGRAVED FOR DR. GORDON'S HISTORY OF THE AMERICAN WAR. T. CONDER SCULPT.
London, [1788]
27 x 17 cm.
In William Gordon, *History of the Rise, Progress, and Establishment of the Independence of the United States*, 4 vols. (London, 1788) 2: opp. 311.
Scale ca. 1:132,000.
Relief shown by hachures.
"Plate III. To face page 310, vol. II."

Copy described. ICN.

Military information. Shows *chevaux de frise* on Hudson River and Harlem Creek, "march of the troops under Gen'l Clinton," and "where Genl. Grant engaged Ld. Stirling."

106

PLAN DER OPERATIONEN DER KÖNIGL. ARMEE UNTER DEM COMMANDO DES GENERALS SIR WILLIAM HOWE IN NEU YORK UND OST NEU JERSEY GEGEN DIE AMERICANISCHE ARMEE UNTER DER ANFÜHRUNG DES GENERAL WASHINGTON VOM 12TEN OCTOBER BIS ZUM 28TEN NOVEMBER 1776 MIT EINER GENAUEN VERSTELLUNG DES GESECHTS AUS DEN WHITE PLAINS DEN 28TEN OCTOBER NACH DEM ENGLISCHEN ORIGINAL VERJUNGT GEZEICHNET VON D. F. SOTZMAN, 1794. C. F. GÜRSCH SC.
[Berlin, 1795]
43 x 30 cm.
In Charles Stedman, *Geschichte des Ursprungs, des Fortgangs, und der Beendigung des amerikanischen Kriegs,* 2 vols. (Berlin: Voss, 1795) 1: at end.
Scale ca. 1: 136,460.
Relief shown by hachures.
Includes references, A, B.
Reduced from the Sauthier-Faden map (map 101).

Copy described. RPJCB.

Military information. As on map 101, second state. British and American units indicated by shading rather than coloring.

Long Island, N. Y.   **27 August 1776**
See also entry: 99, 103–4

107

A PLAN OF NEW YORK ISLAND WITH PART OF LONG ISLAND, STATEN ISLAND & EAST NEW JERSEY, WITH A PARTICULAR DESCRIPTION OF THE ENGAGEMENT ON THE WOODY HEIGHTS OF LONG ISLAND, BETWEEN FLATBUSH AND BROOKLYN, ON THE 27TH OF AUGUST 1776, BETWEEN HIS MAJESTY'S FORCES COMMANDED BY GENERAL HOWE AND THE AMERICANS UNDER MAJOR GENERAL PUTNAM, WITH THE SUBSEQUENT DISPOSITION OF BOTH ARMIES
London: Wm. Faden, Octr. 19th 1776.
48 x 43 cm.

Scale ca. 1:84,000.

Relief shown by hachures; soundings in fathoms.

Includes "references to the Battle of Long Island."

Letterpress below map entitled "An Account of the Proceedings of His Majesty's Forces at the Attack of the Rebel Works on Long Island, on the 27th of August 1776."

A later state was published in Faden's *North American Atlas* (London, 1777), no. 17.

References. Stevens and Tree 41a; Stokes, *Iconography* 1: 353–55; Stokes and Haskell, pp. 49–50. Reproduced in *Atlas of the American Revolution*, no. 12 (later state); Stokes, *Iconography* 1: pl. 45b (4th state).

Variants. Stevens and Tree describe four later states of this plan (41b–41e) and two variant copies, one of which lacks the letterpress account.

Copy described. MiU-C.

Military information. Location of the British fleet is indicated and the five principal ships are named. The various units of both armies are shown by colored rectangles keyed to the "references"; colored, engraved lines show their movements. The letterpress text gives an account of the Battle of Long Island, taken from General Howe's letter to Lord Germain, and numbers of casualties, prisoners, and artillery pieces captured. The account concludes with a narrative of the actions of the British fleet under Commodore Hotham.

108

THE SEAT OF ACTION BETWEEN THE BRITISH AND AMERICAN FORCES OR AN AUTHENTIC PLAN OF THE WESTERN PART OF LONG ISLAND, WITH THE ENGAGEMENT OF THE 27TH AUGUST 1776 BETWEEN THE KING'S FORCES AND THE AMERICANS; CONTAINING ALSO STATEN ISLAND AND THE ENVIRONS OF AMBOY AND NEW YORK, WITH THE COURSE OF HUDSON'S RIVER FROM COURTLAND, THE GREAT MAGAZINE OF THE AMERICAN ARMY, TO SANDY HOOK. FROM THE SURVEYS OF MAJOR HOLLAND

London: Robt. Sayer and Jno. Bennett, 22d Octr. 1776.
46 x 40 cm.
Scale ca. 1:215,000.
Relief shown by hachures.
Inset: "Road from Amboy to Philadelphia."

Copy described. DLC.

Military information. Shows approaches to Brooklyn Heights, position of the Americans, and movements of British fleet in New York harbor. Positions of British and American units are indicated from beginning to end of the Battle of Long Island.

109

PLAN OF THE ATTACK ON THE PROVINCIAL ARMY, ON LONG ISLAND, AUGUST 27TH 1776, WITH THE DRAUGHTS OF NEW YORK ISLAND, STATEN ISLAND, AND THE ADJACENT PART OF THE CONTINENT. BY AN OFFICER OF THE ARMY
[London]: J. Bowles [and] G. Kearseley, Octr. 24th 1776.
37 x 34 cm.
Scale ca. 1:130,300.
Relief shown by hachures.
Includes "explanation" A–F, 1–4.
Serves as the source for a French map (map 112).

Copy described. ICHi.

Military information. The British and American forces are shown, somewhat schematically, as deployed before and after the engagement. The ten lines of "explanation" identify commanders and their maneuvers.

110

TWENTY FIVE MILES ROUND NEW YORK
[London]: W. Hawkes, 1st November 1776.
38 x 38 cm.
Scale ca. 1:211,200.
Includes letterpress text below map entitled "Chronological Table of the Most Interesting Occurrences since the Commencement of Hostilities in North America."

Variants. Stevens and Tree identify four later states (43a–43d). Another state exists (between Stevens and Tree 43a and 43b) that brings the information engraved on the plate down to 13 October 1776. Later states are signed "I. Barber sculp"; the last state was published by Sayer and Bennett, 2 June 1777.

Copy described. MiU-C.

Military information. Indicates sites of engagements on Long Island from 22 August to 3 September. Letterpress includes chronology, from Boston Tea Party through Battle of Long Island, and notes on British military strength. The last state includes a note bringing the military account down to 16 November 1776.

111

A MAP OF THE ISLAND OF NEW YORK AND ENVIRONS, WITH THE MARCH OF THE BRITISH TROOPS. ENGRAVER, TODERICKS WYND

Edinburgh: George Cameron, 14th November 1776.
28 x 33 cm.
Scale ca. 1:200,000.
Soundings in fathoms.
Inset: "A Plan of the City of New York."
"Pr[ice] 1 sh[illing]."

Copy examined. MiU-C.

Military information. Shows the British units, with number or commander indicated, and the fleet offshore.

112

ATTAQUE DE L'ARMÉE DES PROVINCIAUX DANS LONG ISLAND DU 27. AOUST 1776; DESSIN DE L'ISLE DE NEW-YORK ET DES ETATS. PAR UN OFFICIER DE L'ARMÉE. PUBLIÉ À LONDRES PAR ACTE DU PARLEMENT DU 24 8BRE. 1776

Paris: Le Rouge [1776]
36 x 35 cm.
Scale ca. 1:100,000.
Relief shown by hachures.

Includes references A–F, 1–2, 4–7.

Derived from the Bowles and Kearseley map (map 109).

Copy described. DLC.

Military information. British and American forces depicted by rectangular blocks on Long Island, Manhattan Island, and east New Jersey, with references to key.

113

SKETCH OF GENERAL GRANTS POSITION ON LONG ISLAND. ENGRAVED FOR STEDMAN'S HISTORY OF THE AMERICAN WAR

[London, 1794]

35 x 27 cm.

In Charles Stedman, *History of the Origin, Progress, and Termination of the American War*, 2 vols. (London: J. Murray, 1794) 1: opp. 195.

Scale ca. 1:41,000.

Relief shown by hachures.

Includes note concerning Howe's position.

Copy described. ICN.

Military information. The terrain of Woody Heights and the associated ridge across Brooklyn and the passes through it are shown in detail. Troop positions, with names of commanders and lines of march, are indicated.

Kip's Bay, N. Y.   15 September 1776

114

A PLAN OF THE CITY AND ENVIRONS OF NEW YORK IN NORTH AMERICA

[London, November 1776]

29 x 37 cm.

In *Universal Magazine* 59 (1776): opp. 225.

Scale ca. 1:12,750.

Relief shown by hachures.

Letterpress on p. 225: "References to the plan of New-York" A–Z.

Copy described. ICN.

Military information. Two roads are labeled "road to Kepps Bay where the Kings troops landed" and "road to Kings Bridge where the rebels mean to make a stand."

Throg's Point, N. Y. 12–18 October 1776

115

MAP OF NEW YORK I. WITH THE ADJACENT ROCKS AND OTHER REMARKABLE PARTS OF HELL-GATE. BY THOS. KITCHIN SENR. FOR THE LONDON MAGAZINE 1778
[London, 1778]
25 x 19 cm.
In *London Magazine* 47 (1778): before 147.
Scale ca. 1:96,000.
Relief shown pictorially and by hachures.
Prime meridian: London.

Copy described. ICN.

Military information. Indicates "barracks built for American winter quarters, and burnt when the King's troops landed at Frogs Point," and "the ship course" through Hell Gate.

White Plains, N. Y. 28 October 1776
See entry: 94, 99, 101–3, 106

Fort Washington, N. Y. 16 November 1776
See also entry: 101–2

116

A TOPOGRAPHICAL MAP OF THE NORTHN. PART OF NEW YORK ISLAND, EXHIBITING THE PLAN OF FORT WASHINGTON, NOW FORT KNYPHAUSEN, WITH THE REBEL LINES TO THE SOUTHWARD WHICH WERE FORCED BY THE TROOPS UNDER THE COMMAND OF THE RT. HONBLE. EARL PERCY, ON THE 16TH NOVR. 1776, AND SURVEY'D IMMEDIATELY AFTER BY ORDER OF HIS LORDSHIP, BY CLAUDE JOSEPH SAUTHIER. TO WHICH IS ADDED THE ATTACK MADE TO THE NORTHD. BY THE HESSIANS, SUR- ·VEY'D BY ORDER OF LIEUTT. GENL. KNYPHAUSEN
London: Wm. Faden, March 1st 1777.

47 x 26 cm.

Scale ca. 1:21,000.

Relief shown by hachures.

"Published by permission of the Rt. Honble. the Commissioners of Trade & Plantations. By Wm. Faden, 1777."

Includes references A–D, a.

Served as the source for a German map (map 117).

Also published in Faden's *North American Atlas* (London, 1777), no. 18.

References. Stokes, *Iconography* 1:355–56; Stokes and Haskell, p. 52. Reproduced in *American Heritage* 20, no. 5 (August 1969): 31; *Atlas of the American Revolution*, no. 14.

Variants. Two later states are known. The first labels the "Hessian column" and "British column commanded by Earl Percy" and shows four units deployed northwest of Snake Hill; the second appears in Stedman's *History*.

Copy described. RPJCB.

Military information. Shows routes of British and Hessian columns, location of troops. Fort Washington is depicted, as are the American defenses around it. On the New Jersey side Fort Lee is shown with indications of American troops deployed nearby.

117

Grundriss des nördlichen Theils der Neujorks Insel nebst den am 16. Novbr. 1776 eroberten Fort Washington nun das Fort Knÿphausen genannt und dem Fort Lee

[Nuremberg, 1777]

39 x 30 cm.

In [Christoph Heinrich Korn], *Geschichte der Kriege in und ausser Europa*, 30 pts. ([Nuremberg]: Gabriel N. Raspe, 1777–84) 6: opp. 5.

Scale ca. 1:22,080.

Relief shown by hachures.

Derived from the Sauthier-Faden plan of 1 March 1777 (map 116).

Copy described. DLC.

Military information. As on map 116.

NEW JERSEY CAMPAIGN
NOVEMBER 1776–JANUARY 1777
See also entry: 103a

Trenton and Princeton, N. J.
26 December 1776–3 January 1777

118

AN ACCURATE PLAN OF THE COUNTRY BETWEEN NEW YORK AND PHILADELPHIA, WITH THE DISPOSITIONS OF THE FORCES. EXTRACTED FROM THE GAZETTE OF TUESDAY, FEBY. 25TH 1777 [London]: S. Pyle, March 3d 1777.

17 x 29 cm.
Scale ca. 1:450,000.
Oriented with north to the upper right.
Relief shown pictorially and by hachures.
Includes table of distances titled "Road from Philadelphia to New York."
Designed to show British troops in red, Provincials in blue.
"Price 6d."
Very similar to a map published in Dublin in the same year (map 120).

Copy described. NHi.

Military information. Shows troop positions and movements from 28 November 1776 to 4 January 1777. Commanders' names are indicated.

119

PLAN OF THE OPERATIONS OF GENERAL WASHINGTON, AGAINST THE KINGS TROOPS IN NEW JERSEY, FROM THE 26TH OF DECEMBER 1776 TO THE 3D JANUARY 1777. BY WILLIAM FADEN

London: Wm. Faden, 15th April 1777.

29 x 39 cm.

Scale ca. 1:115,000.

Relief shown by hachures.

Includes tables: "Loss in the engagement on the road from Prince Town to Maidenhead, January the 3d 1777," and "Loss at Trenton, December 26th 1776."

Also published in Faden's *North American Atlas* (London, 1777), no. 21.

References. Stevens and Tree 36a. Reproduced in *Atlas of the American Revolution,* no. 15.

Variant. Stevens and Tree identify a later state (36b).

Copy described. DLC.

Military information. Shows "parade of the troops on the evening of the 25th of Decr. 1776." Numerous other such annotations show the routes taken by American forces to Trenton, the action there, and routes through Princeton and Kingston.

120

AN ACCURATE PLAN OF THE COUNTRY BETWEEN NEW YORK AND PHILADELPHIA, WITH THE DISPOSITIONS OF THE FORCES. EXTRACTED FROM THE GAZETTE OF TUESDAY FEBY. 25TH 1777

[Dublin]: I. Exshaw [1777]

17 x 32 cm.

Scale ca. 1:450,000.

Oriented with north to the upper right.

Relief shown pictorially and by hachures.

Includes table of distances titled "Road from Philadelphia to New York."

Possibly published in Exshaw's *Gentleman's and London Magazine.*

Very similar to a map published in London on 3 March 1777 (map 118). This map is extended on the left to show the junction of the Delaware and Schuylkill rivers.

Copy described. N.

Military information. As on map 118.

PHILADELPHIA CAMPAIGN   AUGUST 1777–JUNE 1780
See also entry: 94

121

CARTE DU THEATRE DE LA GUERRE ENTRE LES ANGLAIS ET LES AMÉRICAINS: DRESSÉE D'APRÈS LES CARTES ANGLAISES LES PLUS MODERNES
  Paris: Esnauts et Rapilly, 1777.
  76 x 52 cm.
  Scale ca. 1:1,200,000.
  Prime meridian: London.

Variants. Two later states have been noted. The first, dated 1778, adds a number of place names in New York and New Jersey but does not alter the military information. The second, dated 1782, contains more symbols for deployment of troops outside Philadelphia and at Monmouth, Saratoga, and White Plains.

Copy described. DLC.

Military information. Shows Burgoyne's camp at Saratoga on 16 October 1777 and British forces northwest and southeast of Germantown as well as fortifications on the Delaware River.

122

A CHOROGRAPHICAL MAP OF THE COUNTRY ROUND PHILADELPHIA. BY B. ROMANS
  [New Haven, 1778]
  31 x 34 cm.
  Scale ca. 1:792,000.
  Relief shown pictorially.
  Inset: [Chesapeake Bay]
  Served as the source for a map published in Amsterdam (map 123).

References. Wheat and Brun 304. Reproduced in Guthorn, *American Maps,* p. 31.

Copy described. RPJCB.

Military information. Shows "Grand American Winter Camp January 1778" with small tent symbols, routes of Washington and Howe.

123

A CHOROGRAPHICAL MAP OF THE COUNTRY ROUND PHILADELPHIA. CARTE PARTICULIÈRE DES ENVIRONS DE PHILADELPHIE. H. KLOCKHOFF SCULPS.
> Amsterdam: Covens et Mortier, et Covens, junior [1778?]
> 29 x 33 cm.
> Scale ca. 1:800,000.
> Derived directly from the Romans map (map 122).

Copy described. DLC.

Military information. As on map 122.

124

A PLAN OF THE OPERATIONS OF THE BRITISH & REBEL ARMY IN THE CAMPAIGN, 1777. J. LODGE SCULP.
> [London, 1779]
> 22 x 26 cm.
> In Joseph Galloway, *Letters to a Nobleman on the Conduct of the War* (London: J. Wilkie, 1779), opp. p. 1.
> Scale ca. 1:384,000.
> Oriented with north to the right.
> Inset: "A Plan of Mud Island Fort" (see map 124a).
> Includes references A–I, K–S.

Reference. Reproduced, in part, in Winsor, *Narrative and Critical History* 6: 415.

Copy described. ICN.

Military information. Shows troop locations, lines of march, and "positions which might have been taken" by the British (but were not).

124a

A PLAN OF MUD ISLAND FORT WITH ITS ENVIRONS
[London, 1779]
9 x 11 cm.
Inset on map 124.
Scale ca. 1:75,000.
Includes references A–H.

Reference. Reproduced in Winsor, *Narrative and Critical History* 6: 437.

Military information. Shows batteries, chains, *chevaux de frise*, and "dikes cut by the rebels."

125

A PLAN OF PART OF THE PROVINCES OF PENSYLVANIA AND EAST & WEST NEW JERSEY, SHEWING THE OPERATIONS OF THE ROYAL ARMY UNDER THE COMMAND OF THEIR EXCELLANCIES SIR WILLM. HOWE & SIR HENRY CLINTON, KTS. B., FROM THE LANDING AT ELK RIVER IN 1777, TO THE EMBARKATION AT NAVISINK IN 1778. BY JOHN HILLS, LIEUTT. 23D REGT. & ASST. ENGR.
London: Willm. Faden, June 1st 1784.
23 x 73 cm.
Scale ca. 1:292,000.
Relief shown by hachures.

Copy described. ICN.

Military information. Shows positions of troops, with dates of encampment, and routes. Many individual buildings, including taverns, churches, and meeting halls, are named.

Brandywine, Pa.   11 September 1777

126

BATTLE OF BRANDYWINE, IN WHICH THE REBELS WERE DEFEATED SEPTEMBER THE 11TH 1777, BY THE ARMY UNDER THE COMMAND OF GENERAL SR. WILLM. HOWE. NOTE: THE OPERATIONS OF THE COLUMN UNDER THE COMMAND OF HIS EXCELLANCY LIEUTENANT GENERAL KNYPHAUSEN IS ENGRAVED FROM

A PLAN DRAWN ON THE SPOT BY S. W. WERNER LEIUTT. OF HESSIAN ARTILLERY. ENGRAVED BY WM. FADEN . . . 1778 [London]: Wm. Faden, April 13th 1778.
49 x 44 cm.
Scale ca. 1:16,000.
Relief shown by hachures.
Includes "references to the column under the command of Lt. Genl. Earl Cornwallis" A–H, and, below map, "references to the column under the command of His Excellency Lieutt. Genl. Knyphausen" a-u.

Reference. Reproduced in *Atlas of the American Revolution,* no. 24.

Variant. A later state is known with the imprint date changed to "April 13th 1784."

Copy described. ICN.

Military information. The complex of hills, ravines, and creek beds is carefully delineated (very useful since terrain was important to the outcome). Shows troop positions and movements. British troops are designated by regiment or battalion number. "British," "Hessians and Anspachers," and "Rebels" are indicated by red, blue, and yellow, respectively.

Paoli, Pa.   21 September 1777

127

BRITISH CAMP AT TRUDRUFFRIN FROM THE 18TH TO THE 21ST OF SEPTEMBER 1777, WITH THE ATTACK MADE BY MAJOR GENERAL GREY AGAINST THE REBELS NEAR WHITE HORSE TAVERN ON THE 20TH OF SEPTEMBER. DRAWN BY AN OFFICER ON THE SPOT
[London]: Engrav'd & publish'd by W. Faden, July 1st 1778.
26 x 41 cm.
Scale ca. 1:32,000.
Relief shown by hachures.
Includes "references" A–I, and note.

References. Reproduced in *Pennsylvania Magazine of His-*

tory and Biography 1 (1877): opp. 285; *Atlas of the American Revolution*, no. 25; Winsor, *Narrative and Critical History* 6:424.

Copy described. ICN.

Military information. Detailed plan of the encampment of the British and Hessian troops identified by unit, and Wayne's American force in ambush. The line of march of the British under Grey and Musgrave during their night attack and bayonet charge (familiarly known as the "Paoli Massacre") are indicated, as is the direction of the Americans' retreat westward.

Occupation of Philadelphia 26 September 1777–18 June 1778

128

A PLAN OF THE CITY AND ENVIRONS OF PHILADELPHIA, WITH THE WORKS AND ENCAMPMENTS OF HIS MAJESTY'S FORCES UNDER THE COMMAND OF LIEUTENANT GENERAL SIR WILLIAM HOWE, K.B.
>   London: Engraved and published . . . by Wm. Faden, January 1st 1779.
>   52 x 48 cm.
>   Scale ca. 1:21,000.
>   Relief shown by hachures.
>   Includes "references to the public buildings" A–S.

Reference. Reproduced separately by Historic Urban Plans.

Copy described. ICN.

Military information. Philadelphia was in British hands from 26 September 1777 to 18 June 1778. Shows fortifications, regiments (numbered), and four ships in the harbor. A number of homesteads around the city are named.

Germantown, Pa. 4 October 1777
See also entry:121

129

SKETCH OF THE SURPRISE OF GERMAN TOWN BY THE AMER-

ICAN FORCES COMMANDED BY GENERAL WASHINGTON, OCTOBER
4TH 1777. BY J. HILLS, LT. 23D REGT. & ASST. ENGR.
London: Wm. Faden, March 12th 1784.
46 x 53 cm.
Scale ca. 1:23,500.
Relief shown by hachures.
Includes "references" A–W.

Reference. Reproduced in *Atlas of the American Revolution,*
no. 28.

Copy described. ICN.

Military information. A large-scale, detailed plan with emphasis on complex terrain features. Everything is shown except the dense fog that confused Washington's attacking columns. The lengthy "references" are keyed to the lines of march of the three-pronged attack and the deployment of the defensive forces. Several stages of the engagement are indicated by symbols representing various identified units; names of commanders are given.

Delaware River Forts   10 October–21 November 1777
See also entry: 121, 124a

130

PLAN OF THE CITY AND ENVIRONS OF PHILADELPHIA. SURVEY'D BY N. SCULL AND G. HEAP. ENGRAVED BY WILLM.
FADEN. 1777
London: W. Faden, March 12th 1777.
62 x 46 cm.
Scale ca. 1:43,000.
River soundings in fathoms.
Includes "A table of the distances of the most remarkable places on this plan beginning at the court house," and "Elevation of the State House."
Adapted from a map published in Philadelphia in 1752 (Wheat and Brun 454). Served as the source for maps published in Augsburg, Nuremberg, and Paris (maps 131, 134, 135).
Also published in Faden's *North American Atlas* (London, 1777), no. 23.

References. Stevens and Tree 69b. Reproduced separately by Historic Urban Plans; in *Atlas of the American Revolution*, no. 26 (3d state).

Variants. An earlier state (Stevens and Tree 69a) is without military information as defined in this bibliography. A later state (69c) adds details in the vicinity of the Delaware River forts.

Copy described. KN.

Military information. The third state shows the island between "Hog" and "Mud" islands (now named "Port" Island) heavily fortified as part of the Delaware River defenses of Philadelphia, with number and size of cannon indicated. In addition to the forts at Red Bank and Billingsfort, three double *chevaux de frize* are shown, one connected to Port Island, one to Hog Island, and one from Billingsfort to Billingsfort Island.

131

A PLAN OF THE CITY AND ENVIRONS OF PHILADELPHIA
[Augsburg]: Engraved and published by Matthew Albert Lotter, 1777.
60 x 46 cm.
Scale ca. 1:43,000.
Relief shown by hachures.
Includes an "Elevation of the State House."
Derived directly from the Faden plan of 12 March 1777 (map 130).

Reference. Reproduced in *North American City Plans*, no. 31.

Copy described. ICN.

Military information. Limited to fort on Mud Island and dotted line across river with note: "chevaux de frise which the Americans have laid across to obstruct the navigation."

132

THE COURSE OF DELAWARE RIVER FROM PHILADELPHIA TO CHESTER, EXHIBITING THE SEVERAL WORKS ERECTED BY THE

REBELS TO DEFEND ITS PASSAGE, WITH THE ATTACKS MADE
UPON THEM BY HIS MAJESTY'S LAND AND SEA FORCES
   [London]: William Faden, April 30th 1778.
   45 x 69 cm.
   Scale ca. 1:33,400.
   Relief shown by hachures; soundings in fathoms.
   Insets: "A Sketch of Fort Island" (see map 132a)—"Pro-
      file and Plan of the Sunk Frames or Chevaux de Frize
      which Formed the Stackadoes in the River."

References. Stevens and Tree 17a. Reproduced in *Atlas of
the American Revolution*, no. 29 (2d state).

Variants. Two later states have been recognized, both with
an entirely new inset ("A Plan of Fort Mifflin on Mud Island"
[see map 132b]) and the subtitle changed to . . . *Chester,
with the Several Forts and Stackadoes Raised by the Rebels
and the Attacks Made by His Majesty's Land and Sea Forces.*
The first is dated "March 20th 1779"; the second, "Jany. 1st
1785."

Copy described. DLC.

Military information. The best military map of the fortifications on the Delaware River. The British fleet (named),
American fleet, fortifications on both sides of the river (often with number and size of guns), and two groups of
chevaux de frise and disposition of troops on the Jersey
shore are shown in extraordinary detail.

132a

A SKETCH OF FORT ISLAND
   [London, 30 April 1778]
   15 x 13 cm.
   Inset on map 132.
   Scale ca. 1:8,500.
   Relief shown by hachures.
   Includes references A–E.

Military information. Fort Mifflin is shown by a detailed
ground plan keyed to the references. Four other batteries

are indicated, two giving the number of cannon; an advanced post is shown at northeast end of island.

132b

A PLAN OF FORT MIFFLIN ON MUD ISLAND WITH THE ATTACKS MADE BY THE KING'S TROOPS AND VESSELLS
    25 x 24 cm.
    Inset on later states of map 132.
    Scale ca. 1:6,360.
    Relief shown by hachures.
    Includes references a-f and note.

Military information. This inset is a radical redrawing of map 132a with the outline of the island completely changed. Military information as on map 132a with the addition of extensive stockades outside the fort, two British ships with their lines of fire, and four fortifications on Carpenter's Island with numbers and sizes of guns and lines of fire.

133

A MAP OF THAT PART OF PENSYLVANIA NOW THE PRINCIPLE SEAT OF WAR IN AMERICA, WHEREIN MAY BE SEEN THE SITUATION OF PHILADELPHIA, RED BANK, MUD ISLAND, & GERMANTOWN. FROM AN ACTUAL SURVEY MADE BY NICHOS. SCULL, SURVEYOR OF THE PROVINCE OF PENSYLVANIA. THIS MAP WAS ENGRAVED BY L. JACKSON
    [Dublin, 1778?]
    38 x 30 cm.
    Scale 1:63,360; "an inch to a mile."
    Relief shown pictorially.
    Includes notes on the attack on Fort Mifflin.

Copy described. DLC.

Military information. Limited to the note on the attack and indication of *chevaux de frise.*

134

PLAN DER GEGEND UND STADT VON PHILADELPHIA
    [Nuremberg, 1778]
    36 x 32 cm.

In [Christoph Heinrich Korn], *Geschichte der Kriege in und ausser Europa*, 30 pts. ([Nuremberg]: Gabriel N. Raspe, 1777–84) 6: opp. 128.

Scale ca. 1:57,000.

Table of distances at lower left gives thirty-four locations.

Reduced from the Faden plan of 12 March 1777 (map 130).

Copy described. DLC.

Military information. Shows Delaware River forts, batteries, *chevaux de frise,* etc.

135

ENVIRONS DE PHILADELPHIE. PAR SCULL ET HEAP, PUBLIE A LONDRES PAR FADEN EN 1777. TRADUIT DE L'ANGLAIS

Paris: Le Rouge, 1778.

58 x 45 cm.

In George Louis Le Rouge, *Atlas Ameriquain septentrional* (Paris, 1778).

Scale ca. 1:43,000.

Soundings in fathoms.

Derived directly from the Faden plan of 12 March 1777 (map 130).

Copy described. KN.

Military information. As on map 130.

136

A CHART OF DELAWAR RIVER FROM BOMBAY HOOK TO RIDLEY CREEK, WITH SOUNDINGS &C. TAKEN BY LT. KNIGHT OF THE NAVY. COMPOSED AND PUBLISHED FOR THE USE OF PILOTAGE BY J. F. W. DES BARRES

[London], June 1st 1779.

78 x 56 cm.

In J. F. W. Des Barres, *The Atlantic Neptune,* 4 vols. (London, 1774–82) 4: no. 27.

Scale ca. 1:75,000.

Relief shown by hachures; soundings in fathoms.

Inset: "A Plan of Delawar River from Chester to Philadelphia" (see map 136a).

References. Henry N. Stevens, "Catalogue," no. 159a. Reproduced by Barre Publishers, no. 40.

Variant. Henry N. Stevens, "Catalogue," describes a later state of this plate in which relief is shown more prominently.

Copy described. ICN.

Military information. Limited to inset (see map 136a).

136a

A PLAN OF DELAWAR RIVER FROM CHESTER TO PHILADELPHIA SHEWING THE SITUATION OF HIS MAJESTY'S SHIPS, &C. ON THE 15TH NOVR. 1777. SURVEYED AND SOUNDED BY LIEUTENANT JOHN HUNTER OF THE NAVY
  [London, 1 June 1779]
  78 x 30 cm.
  Inset on map 136.
  Scale ca. 1:29,300.
  Oriented with north toward the upper left.
  Relief shown by hachures; soundings in fathoms.
  Includes "references" A–I, K–N.

Military information. Shows positions of ships, batteries, *chevaux de frise*, etc.

FINAL ENGAGEMENTS IN THE NORTH
MARCH 1778–JUNE 1780
Quintan's Bridge, N. J.   18 March 1778

137

AFFAIR AT QUINTIN'S BRIDGE, 18TH MARCH 1778. FROM A SKETCH BY LT. COLL. SIMCOE, TAKEN ON THE SPOT. COPY G. SPENCER LT. Q. RS.
  [Exeter, 1787]
  18 x 21 cm.
  In John G. Simcoe, *A Journal of the Operations of the Queen's Rangers* (Exeter, Eng., [1787]), opp. p. 26.
  Scale ca. 1:12,200.
  Relief shown by hachures.
  Includes references A–I.

Copy described. ICN.

Military information. As with several of the other battle plans accompanying Simcoe's *Journal*, this is a splendid, large-scale, detailed plan of one of the less important engagements of the war. The deployment of American and British units is indicated, keyed to references that give further details. Lines of march are shown, and terrain features are prominently displayed.

Hancock's Bridge, N. J.   21 March 1778
138

SURPRIZE OF REBELS AT HANCOCKS HOUSE. FROM A SKETCH BY LT. COL. SIMCOE TAKEN ON THE SPOT. COPY G. SPENCER LT. Q. RS.
> [Exeter, 1787]
> 19 x 21 cm.
> In John G. Simcoe, *A Journal of the Operations of the Queen's Rangers* (Exeter, Eng., [1787]), opp. p. 28.
> Scale not indicated.
> Relief shown by hachures.
> Includes references outside map border, A–G.

Copy described. ICN.

Military information. See annotation for map 137.

Barren Hill, Pa.   20 May 1778
139

SKETCH OF FAYETTE'S POSITION AT BARREN HILL. ENGRAVED FOR STEDMANS HISTORY OF THE AMERICAN WAR
> [London, 1794]
> 22 x 17 cm.
> In Charles Stedman, *History of the Origin, Progress, and Termination of the American War*, 2 vols. (London: J. Murray, 1794) 1: opp. 377.
> Scale not indicated.
> Oriented with north toward the upper right.
> Relief shown by hachures.
> Includes "references" A–G.

Copy described. ICN.

Military information. The seven references describe the action that the indication of relief helps to interpret. Locations of British and American forces at the outset are depicted.

Monmouth, N. J.   29 June 1778
140

PLAN DE LA BATAILLE DE MONTMOUTH OÙ LE GL. WASHINGTON COMMANDAIT L'ARMEÉ AMÉRICAINE ET LE GL. CLINTON L'ARMÉE ANGLAISE, LE 28 JUIN 1778
  [Brussels, 1782]
  22 x 39 cm.
  In Michel René Hilliard D'Auberteuil, *Essais historiques et politiques sur les Anglo-Américains,* 2 vols. and atlas. (Brussels, 1782), atlas.
  Scale ca. 1:31,000.
  Oriented with north toward the upper left.
  Relief shown by hachures.
  The lower half of the sheet contains "explication des chifres" a, 1–22.

References. Reproduced in *Atlas of the American Revolution,* no. 30; in part, in Winsor, *Narrative and Critical History* 6:444.

Copy described. ICN.

Military information. The only contemporaneously published plan of this, the last major confrontation of the British and American armies in the northern theater. The deep ravines that figured importantly are carefully drawn, as are the several positions taken up by both armies. Considerable detail is supplied by the 23-item explanation accompanying the map.

Sandy Hook, N. J.   11–22 July 1778
141

PLAN OF THE SITUATION OF THE FLEET WITHIN SANDY HOOK. JN. LODGE SCULP.
  London: J. Almon, Feby. 3d 1779.
  39 x 38 cm.

In [Thomas L. O'Beirne], *A Candid and Impartial Narrative*, 2d ed. (London: J. Almon, [1779]), opp. p. 3.
Scale ca. 1:43,000.
Oriented with north to the left.
Relief shown by hachures; soundings in fathoms.
Includes an "explanation of the plate" on page 3.

Copy described. ICN.

Military information. The depth soundings, coastline, and the bars blocking the entrance of D'Estaing's fleet to engage Admiral Howe's ships are all shown in detail. Positions of both fleets are indicated, and the British ships are named on the plan.

King's Bridge, N. Y. 31 August 1778
See also entry: 114

142

AMBUSCADE OF THE INDIANS AT KINGSBRIDGE, AUGUST 31ST 1778. FROM A SKETCH BY LT. COL: SIMCOE, TAKEN ON THE SPOT. COPY G. SPENCER LT. QS. RS.
[Exeter, 1787]
18 x 23 cm.
In John G. Simcoe, *A Journal of the Operations of the Queen's Rangers* (Exeter, Eng., [1787]), opp. p. 54.
Scale not indicated.
Relief shown by hachures.
Includes references A–I.

Copy described. ICN.

Military information. See annotation for map 137.

Babcock's House, N. Y. September 1778

143

MARCH OF THE QUEENS RANGERS, EMMERICKS CORPS, THE CAVALRY OF THE LEGION UNDER LT. COL. TARLETON, AND A DETACHMENT OF THE YAGERS, THE WHOLE COMMANDED BY LT. COL: SIMCOE TO SURPRIZE A CORPS OF REBEL LIGHT TROOPS UNDER COL: GIST

[Exeter, 1787]

16 x 20 cm.

In John G. Simcoe, *A Journal of the Operations of the Queen's Rangers* (Exeter, Eng., [1787]), opp. p. 56.

Scale not indicated.

Relief shown by hachures.

Includes "explanation" A–H.

Copy described. ICN.

Military information. See annotation for map 137.

Oyster Bay, N. Y.   November 1778–May 1779

144

PLAN OF OYSTER BAY, AS FORTIFIED BY THE QUEEN'S RANGERS. FROM A SKETCH BY LT. COL. SIMCOE, TAKEN ON THE SPOT. COPY G. SPENCER LT. Q. RS.

[Exeter, 1787]

20 x 24 cm.

In John G. Simcoe, *A Journal of the Operations of the Queen's Rangers* (Exeter, Eng., [1787]), opp. p. 62.

Scale ca. 1:11,100.

Relief shown by hachures.

Includes references A–E.

Copy described. ICN.

Military information. Gives details of fortification and quarters of Simcoe's troops taken up on Long Island during the winter of 1778–79.

Stoney Point, N. Y.   16 July 1779

145

A PLAN OF THE SURPRISE OF STONEY POINT BY A DETACHMENT OF THE AMERICAN ARMY COMMANDED BY BRIGR. GENL. WAYNE, ON THE 15TH JULY 1779. ALSO OF THE WORKS ERECTED ON VERPLANKS POINT FOR THE DEFENCE OF KINGS FERRY, BY THE BRITISH FORCES IN JULY, 1779. FROM THE SURVEYS OF WM. SIMPSON, LT. 17TH RT. AND D. CAMPBELL, LT. 42D RT. BY JOHN HILLS, LT. 23D REGT. & ASST. ENGR.

London: Printed for Wm. Faden, March 1st 1784.
50 x 70 cm.
Scale ca. 1:5,500.
Relief shown by shading.
Includes a note on the cannon in Fort Fayette and "references to Stoney Point" 1–5, A–I.

Reference. Reproduced in *Atlas of the American Revolution*, no. 32.

Copy described. ICN.

Military information. The defenses of the strong points at either end of King's Ferry on the Hudson are carefully drawn, as are the relief features. The silent line of march of Anthony Wayne's nocturnal assault force is shown to where they made the bayonet charge that avenged Wayne's drubbing at Paoli.

Springfield, N. J.   7–23 June 1780

146

SKETCH OF THE POSITION OF THE BRITISH FORCES AT ELIZABETH TOWN POINT AFTER THEIR RETURN FROM CONNECTICUT FARM IN THE PROVINCE OF EAST JERSEY UNDER THE COMMAND OF HIS EXCELLY. LEIUTT. GENL. KNYPHAUSEN, ON THE 8TH JUNE 1780. BY JOHN HILLS, LIEUTT. 23D REGT. & ASST. ENGR.
London: Willm. Faden, April 12th 1784.
62 x 52 cm.
Scale ca. 1:7,100.
Oriented with north toward the upper right.
Relief shown by shading.
Includes "references" A–H.

Reference. Reproduced in *Atlas of the American Revolution*, no. 33.

Copy described. ICN.

Military information. Depicts at large scale the British and Hessian forces, naming the units and commanders. Shows the fortifications and bridge of boats used for the retreat to Staten Island.

5

THE WAR IN
THE WEST INDIES

Dominica   8 September 1778

147

CARTE DE LA DOMINIQUE PRISE PAR LE FRANCOIS LE 7 SEPTEM-
BRE 1778. AVEC LE PLAN DU DEBARQUEMENT, ET DE L'ATTAQUE
DES FORTS ET BATTERIES PAR LES TROUPES ET LES FRÉGATES
DE SA MAJESTÉ . . . PAR LE S. BUACHE
   Paris: l'auteur, 1778.
   62 x 48 cm.
   Scale ca. 1:65,770.
   Relief shown by hachures.
   Prime meridians: Paris and Ferro.
   Insets: "Plan du débarquement et de l'attaque des forts
      et batteries" (see map no. 147a)—[Lesser Antilles from
      Antigua to Grenada].
   "Dédiée a M. de Sartine."

Copy described. DLC.

Military information. Shows roads, defensive batteries, and
artillery magazines around Prince Rupert Bay.

147a

PLAN DU DEBARQUEMENT ET DE L'ATTAQUE DES FORTS ET
BATTERIES
   [Paris, 1778]
   20 x 17 cm.
   Inset on map no. 147.
   Scale ca. 1:60,275.
   Relief shown by hachures.
   Includes references, 1–9.

Military information. Shows ships offshore (four are named), positions of shore batteries with lines of fire, and place where troops disembarked and deployed on land.

Saint Lucia   12–28 December 1778
148

PLAN OF ST. LUCIA IN THE WEST INDIES SHEWING THE POSITIONS OF THE ENGLISH & FRENCH FORCES WITH THE ATTACKS MADE AT ITS REDUCTION IN DECR. 1778. T. BOWEN SCT.
   [London, April 1779]
   19 x 26 cm.
   In *Gentleman's Magazine* 49 (1779): opp. 184.
   Scale ca. 1:52,000.
   Oriented with north at the left.
   Relief shown by hachures.

Reference. Reproduced in Begnaud, p. 80.

Copy described. DLC.

Military information. Shows the west coast of the island from Gros Inlet Bay to Le Grand Cul de Sac, with land batteries and troop positions indicated.

149

ATTACKS OF ST. LUCIE WITH THE BLOCKADE OF THE FRENCH FLEET UNDER COUNT D'ESTAING IN MARTINICO BY ADMIRAL BYRONS FLEET
   [London]: John Bowles, 1st May 1779.
   24 x 34 cm.
   Scale ca. 1:50,000.
   Oriented with north at the left.
   Relief shown by hachures.
   Inset: [Saint Lucia Channel] (see map 149a).
   Includes "reference to the blockade" A–D.

Reference. Reproduced in *Atlas of the American Revolution,* no. 34.

Copy described. DLC.

Military information. Ships of both fleets are depicted with their lines of fire; many are named. Land batteries are indicated and the disposition of the various French and English military units shown by rectangles, identified by commanders. Several legends on map relate the naval and military proceedings from 13 to 16 December 1778.

149a

[SAINT LUCIA CHANNEL]
  [London, 1st May 1779]
  13 x 10 cm.
  Inset on map 149.
  Scale ca. 1:1,250,000.
  Relief shown by hachures.
  Prime meridian: Ferro.

Military information. Shows shore batteries at the south end of Martinique and around Port Royal Harbor. The French and British fleets are shown pictorially.

150

SKETCH OF PART OF THE ISLAND OF STE. LUCIE
  London: Wm. Faden, Nov. 5, 1781.
  38 x 48 cm.
  Scale ca. 1:30,000; "Computed at about 2500 feet to 1 inch."
  Oriented with north toward the left.
  Relief shown by hachures.
  Includes "references" A–F, 1–6, 8–9.
  Tables list "the French ships of the line," "British troops employed on this service," and "names of the people whose houses are marked on the plan."
  Also published in Colin Lindsay, *Extracts from Colonel Tempelhoffe's History*, 2 vols. (London: T. Cadell, 1793) 2: opp. 441.

Variants. Variant copies exist with a letterpress account, extracted from General Grant's letter of 31 December 1778, printed below the map. There is also a later state with the imprint "London, Published by James Wyld [n.d.]."

Copy described. NHi.

Military information. A detailed plan. Shows locations of

land forces, size of cannon in the French batteries, locations of the fleets (Admiral Barrington's ships are named), and "track of the Count d'Estaing." The tables indicate commanders, numbers of guns and men.

Grenada   4 July 1779

151

PLAN OF THE FRENCH ATTACKS UPON THE ISLAND OF GRENADA, WITH THE ENGAGEMENT BETWEEN THE ENGLISH FLEET UNDER THE COMMAND OF ADMIRAL BYRON AND THE FRENCH FLEET UNDER COUNT D'ESTAING. DRAWN BY AN OFFICER ON BOARD THE FLEET, JULY 1779. J. LUFFMAN SC.
   London: T. Harris, 21 Sept. 1779.
   24 x 37 cm.
   Scale ca. 1:13,400.
   Oriented with north toward the left.
   Includes seventeen lines of notes.

References. Reproduced in Begnaud, p. 93. *Atlas of the American Revolution*, no. 35.

Copy described. DLC.

Military information. Both fleets depicted by detailed drawings of individual ships; locates military units and fortifications on land. The maneuvers of land and naval forces are detailed in the lengthy notes.

152

PLAN OF THE ACTION OFF GRENADA ON THE 6TH OF JULY 1779. 1ST POSITION AT 5 A.M. [2D POSITION AT 15 MINUTES PAST 7 A.M.—3D POSITION AT 8 A.M.—4TH POSITION AT HALF PAST 10 A.M.—5TH POSITION AT 3 A.M. (*sic*)]. J. MATTHEWS DELIN. J. HUNTER SCULP.
   [Chester, Eng., 1784]
   5 maps 19 x 28 cm.
   In [John Matthews], *Twenty-one Plans, with Explanations, of Different Actions in the West Indies* (Chester, Eng.: J. Fletcher, 1784), nos. 1–5.

Scales ca. 1:75,000.
Oriented with north to the left.
Relief shown pictorially.
The first three maps include one column of "reference"
to the British fleet, another to the French. The last two
sheets include one column of "reference" to both fleets.
Served as the source for maps published in Amsterdam
(entry 153).

Reference. Reproduced in Begnaud, pp. 110–14.

Copy described. DLC.

Military information. The first three maps show the same
part of the west coast of the island with the successive positions of the fleets. British ships are colored red or blue to
indicate squadron. The fourth map shows the fleets engaged
further north along the coast, and no land is shown on the
fifth map. Wind directions are indicated.

153

PLAN VAN DE ACTIE BY GRENADA, OP DEN 6 JULY 1779. EERSTE
POSITIE. [15 MINUTEN OVER ZEVENEN.—DERDE POSITIE.—OM
HALF ELF UUREN.—VYFDE POSITIE]
[Amsterdam, 1791]
5 maps ca. 19 x 31 cm.
In [John Matthews], *Korte verklaringe van verscheidene
actiën, tusschen de Engelsche en Fransche vlooten . . .
in de West-Indiën* (Amsterdam: Gerard Hulst van
Keulen, 1791), nos. 1–5.
Scales ca. 1:75,000.
Oriented with north to the left.
Relief shown pictorially.
Derived directly from maps in the English edition (entry
152).

Copy described. MiU-C.

Military information. As in entry 152.

Basseterre, Saint Kitts   22 July 1779

154

PLAN OF THE SITUATION OF THE BRITISH FLEET AT ANCHOR
OFF BASSETERRE ON THE 22D JULY 1779. J. MATTHEWS DELIN.
J. HUNTER SCULP.
 [Chester, Eng., 1784]
 19 x 28 cm.
 In [John Matthews], *Twenty-one Plans, with Explana-
  tions, of Different Actions in the West Indies* (Chester,
  Eng.: J. Fletcher, 1784), no. 6.
 Scale ca. 1:20,800.
 Oriented with north to the left.
 Relief shown pictorially.
 Includes a four-line "reference" to the fleets.
 Served as the source for a map published in Amsterdam
  (map 155).

Reference. Reproduced in Begnaud, p. 117.

Copy described. DLC.

Military information. Shows the town and fort of Basseterre
with the British and French fleets offshore. Wind direction
is indicated, and British ships are colored red or blue to
indicate squadron.

155

PLAN VAN DE LEGGINGE DER ENGELSCHE VLOOT TEN ANKER OF
EN AAN VAN BASSETERRE DEN 22 JULY 1779
 [Amsterdam, 1791]
 19 x 31 cm.
 In [John Matthews], *Korte verklaringe van verscheidene
  actiën, tusschen de Engelsche en Fransche vlooten . . .
  in de West-Indiën* (Amsterdam: Gerard Hulst van Keu-
  len, 1791), no. 6.
 Scale ca. 1:21,000.
 Oriented with north to the left.
 Relief shown pictorially.
 Derived directly from a map in the English edition (map
  154).

Copy described. MiU-C.

Military information. As on map 154.

Omoa, Honduras 17 October 1779

156

WEST INDIES, WITH THE HARBOUR & FORT OF OMOA, FROM THE
BEST AUTHORITIES
[London, March 1780]
30 x 64 cm.
In *Political Magazine* 1 (1780): opp. 225.
Scale ca. 1:9,750,000.
Relief shown pictorially.
Inset: "The Harbour & Fort of Omoa" (see map 156a).

Copy described. ICN.

Military information. Limited to inset (see map 156a).

156a

THE HARBOUR & FORT OF OMOA
10 x 9 cm.
Inset on map 156.
Scale ca. 1:31,500.
Oriented with north to the left.
Relief shown by hachures.

Military information. Four named ships are shown firing
at the fort.

Martinique 29 April 1781

157

[PLANS OF THE ACTION OFF MARTINIQUE] 1ST POSITION AT 7
A.M. [2D POSITION 15 MINUTES PAST 10 A.M.—3D POSITION
AT 11 A.M.] J. MATTHEWS DELIN. J. HUNTER SCULP.
[Chester, Eng., 1784]
3 maps 19 x 28 cm.
In [John Matthews], *Twenty-one Plans, with Explana-
tions, of Different Actions in the West Indies* (Chester,
Eng.: J. Fletcher, 1784), nos. 7–9.

Scales ca. 1:152,000.
Oriented with north to the left.
Relief shown pictorially.
Each map contains one column of "reference" to the British fleet and another to the French.
Served as the source for maps published in Amsterdam (entry 159).

Reference. Reproduced in Begnaud, pp. 218–20.

Copy described. DLC.

Military information. The mainland from north of Fort Royal to Cape Diamond is shown on each map, with the disposition of the fleets. Wind direction is indicated, and British ships are colored red or blue to indicate the squadron.

158

SJÖ-BATAILLON D. 29 APRILL 1781. EMELLEN FRANSKA AMIRALEN GREFVE GRASSE OCH DEN ENGELSKA AMIRALEN SAMUEL HOOD, IFRÅN K: 10 FÖR MIDDAGEN TILL K. ½ 3 EFTER MIDDAGEN. TAB. I
[Stockholm, 1787]
18 x 30 cm.
In [Carl Gustaf Tornquist], *Grefve Grasses siö-batailler* (Stockholm: Joh. Christ. Holmberg, 1787).
Scale ca. 1:170,000.
Relief shown by hachures.
Includes references a-g.

Reference. Reproduced in Tornquist, *Naval Campaigns*, p. 173.

Copy described. RPJCB.

Military information. Shows ship positions and movements; wind direction.

159

[PLANS OF THE ACTION OFF MARTINIQUE]. EERSTE POSITIE. [TWEEDE POSITIE, 15 MINUTEN OVEN TIENEN.—DERDE POSITIE, VAN DEN ELFDEN]

[Amsterdam, 1791]
3 maps ca. 19 x 31 cm.
In [John Matthews], *Korte verklaringe van verscheidene actiën, tusschen de Engelsche en Fransche vlooten . . . in de West-Indien* (Amsterdam: Gerard Hulst van Keulen, 1791), nos. 7–9.
Scales ca. 1:150,000.
Oriented with north to the left.
Relief shown pictorially.
Derived directly from maps in the English edition (entry 157).

Copy described. MiU-C.

Military information. As in entry 157.

Saint Kitts   11 January–12 February 1782

160

AN ACCURATE MAP OF THE ISLANDS OF ST. CHRISTOPHERS AND NEVIS IN THE WEST INDIES. BY AN OFFICER. WITH THE POSITION OF THE ENGLISH AND FRENCH FLEETS, FEBRUARY 7TH 1782. J. CARY SC.
[London]: I. Fielding, J. Sewell, J. Debrett, April 1, 1782.
32 x 39 cm.
In *European Magazine* 1 (1782): opp. 187.
Scale ca. 1:162,500.
Relief shown by hachures.

Copy described. ICN.

Military information. "The French fleet" and "Adl. Hoods squadron" are shown pictorially.

161

[PLANS OF THE BATTLES OFF SAINT KITTS] 1ST POSITION AT NOON. [2D POSITION AT ½ PAST 3 A.M.—POSITION ON THE 26TH] J. MATTHEWS DELIN. J. HUNTER SCULP.
[Chester, Eng., 1784]
3 maps 19 x 28 cm.
In [John Matthews], *Twenty-one Plans, with Explanations, of Different Actions in the West Indies* (Chester, Eng.: J. Fletcher, 1784), nos. 10–12.

Scales ca. 1:36,200.
Oriented with north to the left.
Relief shown pictorially.
The first and third maps contain one column of "reference" to the British and French fleets; the second map has a separate column for each fleet.
Served as the source for maps published in Amsterdam (entry 163).

Reference. Reproduced in Begnaud, pp. 248–50.

Copy described. DLC.

Military information. The three maps show the northward trend of the fleets from Dogwood Point at the southern end of Nevis on the first sheet, to Horseshoe Point and the Narrows on the second sheet, and South Friar's Bay on the last sheet. Wind directions are indicated, and British ships are colored red or blue to indicate squadron.

162

ATTAQUEN VID ÖN ST. CHRISTOPHER AF GREFVE GRASSE MOT AMIRAL HOOD D: 25 OCH 26 JANU: 1781 [I.E., 1782] UNDER FÄSTNINGENS BELÄGRANDE. TAB. III
[Stockholm, 1787]
18 x 30 cm.
In [Carl Gustaf Tornquist], *Grefve Grasses siö-batailler* (Stockholm: Joh. Christ. Holmberg, 1787).
Scale ca. 1:51,000.
Relief shown by hachures.
Includes references, a-e.

Reference. Reproduced in Tornquist, *Naval Campaigns*, p. 177.

Copy described. RPJCB.

Military information. Shows ship positions and movements; wind direction.

163

[PLANS OF THE BATTLES OFF SAINT KITTS]. EERSTE POSITIE

OP DEN MIDDAG. [TWEEDE POSITIE OM HALF VIER UUREN.—DE
DERDE POSITIE OP DEN 26TEN]
[Amsterdam, 1791]
3 maps ca. 19 x 31 cm.
In [John Matthews], *Korte verklaringe van verscheidene
actiën, tusschen de Engelsche en Fransche vlooten* . . .
in de West-Indiën (Amsterdam: Gerard Hulst van
Keulen, 1791), nos. 10–12.
Scales ca. 1:36,000.
Oriented with north to the left.
Relief shown pictorially.
Derived directly from maps in the English edition (entry
161).

Copy described. MiU-C.

Military information. As in entry 161.

Saint's Passage   9–12 April 1782

164

[PLANS OF THE BATTLE OF THE SAINTS]. PREMIERE POSITION
AU LEVER DU SOLEIL. [DEUXIEME POSITION.—TROISIEME POSI-
TION À 8 HEURES.—QUATRIEME POSITION À 8 HEURES ET ¼.
—CINQUIEME POSITION A 10 HEURES.—SIXIEME POSITION À 11
HEURES ET DEMIE.—SEPTIEME POSITION À 3 HEURES ET ½ DU
SOIR.—HUITIEME POSITION À 7 HEURES DU SOIR]
[Paris, 1782]
8 maps ca. 41 x 52 cm.
In François J. Paul, marquis de Grasse-Tilly, *Memoiré du
comte de Grasse, sur le combat naval du 12 avril 1782*
([Paris, 1782]), at end.
Scales ca. 1:86,000.
Oriented with north toward the upper left.
Most sheets signed "Dupuis sculp. Thuillier scripsit."
Some sheets have "renvois" for identifying ships.
Served as the sources for maps published in the Dutch
edition (entry 165).

References. Reproduced in Begnaud, pp. 258–65; as Massachusetts Historical Society, Americana Series, no. 211.

Copy described. DLC.

Military information. All maps cover basically the same area. Ships are shown pictorially, sometimes with lines of fire and billowing smoke. Wind directions are indicated.

165

PLAN VAN DE ACTIE OP DEN 12 APRIL 1782 IN DE WEST-INDIËN VOORGEVALLEN. EERSTE POSITIE MET ZONS OPGANG. [TWEEDE POSITIE.—DERDE POSITIE TEN ACHT UUREN.—VIERDE POSITIE QUARTIER OVER ACHTEN.—VYFDE POSITIE OM TIEN UUR.—ZESDE POSITIE TEN HALF TWAALF.—ZEEVENDE POSITIE 'S NAMIDDAGS TEN HALF VIER UUR.—ACHTSTE POSITIE 'S AVONDS OM 7 UUR]

> [Amsterdam, 1782]
> 8 maps ca. 31 x 44 cm.
> In François J. Paul, marquis de Grasse-Tilly, *Memorie van den Graave de Grasse betreffende de actien in de West-Indiën voorgevallen* ([Amsterdam, 1782]), at end.
> Scales ca. 1:105,000.
> Oriented with north toward the upper left.
> Most sheets include "renvoi[s]" for identifying ships.
> Derived directly from the maps published in the French edition (entry 164).

Copy described. RPJCB.

Military information. As in entry 164, except ships are shown in plan view, not pictorially.

166

PLAN OF THE ACTION ON THE 9TH OF APRIL 1782. 1ST POSITION AT 6 A.M. [2D POSITION 45 MINUTES PAST 9.—3D POSITION AT NOON] J. MATTHEWS DELIN. J. HUNTER SCULP.

> [Chester, Eng., 1784]
> 3 maps 19 x 29 cm.
> In [John Matthews], *Twenty-one Plans, with Explanations, of Different Actions in the West Indies* (Chester, Eng.: J. Fletcher, 1784), nos 13–15.
> Scales ca. 1:61,700.

Oriented with north to the left.

Relief shown pictorially.

Each sheet contains a column of "reference" to the fleets.

Served as the source for maps published in Amsterdam
(entry 173).

Reference. Reproduced in Begnaud, pp. 266–68.

Copy described. DLC.

Military information. The maps show the location of the
fleets off the northwest coast of Dominica ("Isle of Domin-
aco"). Wind directions are indicated, and British ships are
colored red or blue to indicate squadron.

167

PLAN OF THE ACTION ON THE 12TH OF APRIL 1782. 1ST POSI-
TION AT 6 A.M. [2D POSITION 15 MINUTES PAST 7 A.M.—3D
POSITION AT 10 A.M.—4TH POSITION AT NOON.—5TH POSITION
AT 3 A.M.—6TH POSITION AT SUNSET] J. MATTHEWS DELIN.
J. HUNTER SCULP.

[Chester, Eng., 1784]

6 maps 19 x 29 cm.

In [John Matthews], *Twenty-one Plans, with Explanations, of Different Actions in the West Indies* (Chester,
Eng.: J. Fletcher, 1784), nos. 16–21.

Scales ca. 1:61,700.

Oriented with north to the left.

Relief shown pictorially.

Each sheet contains a column of "reference" to the fleets.

Served as the source for maps published in Amsterdam
(entry 174).

Reference. Reproduced in Begnaud, pp. 269–74.

Copy described. DLC.

Military information. The final phases of the battle of Saint's
Passage. The first five maps show the fleets off the northwest
coast of Dominica. On the sixth sheet, no land is shown.
Wind directions are indicated, and British ships are colored
red or blue to indicate their squadron.

168

PLAN CHARTA ÖFVER EN DEL AF LOFWART ÖARNE, TJENANDA
TILL UPLYSNING ÖFVER BESHRIFVNINGEN AF COMBATTERNE D:
9 OCH 12 APRILL 1782. SAINTE LUCIE OCH ANTIGUE DÅ TILL-
HÖRIGE ENGELSKA KRONAU. TAB. V
[Stockholm, 1787]
19 x 30 cm.
In [Carl Gustaf Tornquist], *Grefve Grasses siö-batailler*
(Stockholm: Joh. Christ. Holmberg, 1787).
Scale ca. 1:1,050,000.
Relief shown by hachures.

Reference. Reproduced in Tornquist, *Naval Campaigns*, p.
181.

Copy described. RPJCB.

Military information. Shows the course of the fleets through
the islands by dotted lines.

169

ACTION D: 9 APRIL 1782 OM EFTERMIDDAGEN. TAB. IV
[Stockholm, 1787]
18 x 31 cm.
In [Carl Gustaf Tornquist], *Grefve Grasses siö-batailler*
(Stockholm: Joh. Christ. Holmberg, 1787).
Scale ca. 1:150,000.
Relief shown by hachures.
Includes references a-h.

Reference. Reproduced in Tornquist, *Naval Campaigns*, p.
179.

Copy described. RPJCB.

Military information. Shows ship positions and movements;
wind direction.

170

ACTION D. 12 APRILL 1782. 1STA. STALLNINGEN VID COMBATTENS
BÖRGAN K: ¼ 2 OM MORGONEN, ARRIERE GUARDIE UTI TETEN
[Stockholm, 1787]
18 x 29 cm.

In [Carl Gustaf Tornquist], *Grefve Grasses siö-batailler* (Stockholm: Joh. Christ. Holmberg, 1787).

Scale not indicated.

Relief shown by hachures.

Includes references A–F, H, K–M, O.

Reference. Reproduced in Tornquist, *Naval Campaigns,* p. 183.

Copy described. RPJCB.

Military information. Shows ship positions and movements; wind direction.

171

ACTION D: 12 APRILL 2DRA. STÄLLNINGEN K: ½ 11 DÅ VINDEN ÄNDRAT SIG TILL SYD OST. TAB. VII

[Stockholm, 1787]

18 x 30 cm.

In [Carl Gustaf Tornquist], *Grefve Grasses siö-batailler* (Stockholm: Joh. Christ. Holmberg, 1787).

Scale not indicated.

Includes references a-d, f-i.

Reference. Reproduced in Tornquist, *Naval Campaigns,* p. 185.

Copy described. RPJCB.

Military information. Shows ship positions and movements; wind directions.

172

ACTION D: 12 APRILL 3DE. STÄLNINGEN OM EFTERMIDDAGEN K: EMELLAN 2 OCH 3 SEDAN VINDEN ALDELES STILNAT UT. TAB. VIII

[Stockholm, 1787]

18 x 30 cm.

In [Carl Gustaf Tornquist], *Grefve Grasses siö-batailler* (Stockholm: Joh. Christ. Holmberg, 1787).

Scale not indicated.

Includes references a-t, v, x, z.

Reference. Reproduced in Tornquist, *Naval Campaigns,* p. 187.

Copy described. RPJCB.

Military information. Shows ship positions and movements; wind direction.

173

PLAN VAN DE ACTIE, VOORGEVALLEN OP DEN 9DEN APRIL 1782. EERSTE POSITIE. [TWEEDE POSITIE 45 MINUTEN OVER 9.— DERDE POSITIE OP DEN MIDDAG]
[Amsterdam, 1791]
3 maps ca. 19 x 31 cm.
In [John Matthews], *Korte verklaringe van verscheidene actiën, tusschen de Engelsche en Fransche vlooten . . . in de West-Indiën* (Amsterdam: Gerard Hulst van Keulen, 1791), nos. 13–15.
Scales ca. 1:62,000.
Oriented with north to the left.
Relief shown pictorially.
Derived directly from maps in the English edition (entry 166).

Copy described. MiU-C.

Military information. As in entry 166.

174

PLAN VAN DE ACTIE VOORGEVALLEN DEN 12DEN APRIL 1782. EERSTE POSITIE. [TWEEDE POSITIE 15 MINUTEN OVER ZEEVEN. —DERDE POSITIE OM TIEN UUREN.—VIERDE POSITIE OP DEN MIDDAG.—DE VYFDE POSITIE OM DRIE UUREN.—SESDE POSITIE MET ZONS ONDERGANG]
[Amsterdam, 1791]
6 maps ca. 19 x 31 cm.
In [John Matthews], *Korte verklaringe van verscheidene actiën, tusschen de Engelsche en Fransche vlooten . . . in de West-Indiën* (Amsterdam: Gerard Hulst van Keulen, 1791), nos. 16–21.
Scales ca. 1:62,000.
Oriented with north to the left.
Relief shown pictorially.

Derived directly from maps in the English edition (entry 167).

Copy described. MiU-C.

Military information. As in entry 167.

6

VIRGINIA CAMPAIGNS

Richmond, Va. 5 January 1781

175

SKIRMISH AT RICHMOND, JAN. 5TH 1781. FROM A SKETCH OF
LT. ALLANS OF THE QUEENS RANGERS
[Exeter, 1787]
16 x 20 cm.
In John G. Simcoe, *A Journal of the Operations of the
Queen's Rangers* (Exeter, Eng., [1787]), opp. p. 112.
Scale ca. 1:35,000.
Relief shown by hachures.
Includes references A–F.

Reference. Verner, *Yorktown Campaign* IV.

Copy described. ICN.

Military information. Gives the plan of the town, surrounding terrain, and the adjacent stretch of the James River.
Shows the deployment of six groups of British and American troops, with colors used to distinguish the Queen's
Rangers, the Hessians, the Rebels, etc.

Burrell's, Va. 17 April 1781

176

THE LANDING AT BURRELL'S, APRIL 17TH 1781. TAKEN ON THE
SPOT BY G. SPENCER LT. Q. R.
[Exeter, 1787]
19 x 24 cm.
In John G. Simcoe, *A Journal of the Operations of the
Queen's Rangers* (Exeter, Eng., [1787]), opp. p. 132.

Scale ca. 1:22,000.
Relief shown by hachures.
Includes references A–E.

Reference. Verner, *Yorktown Campaign* V.

Copy described. ICN.

Military information. Shows the lines of movement of the British ships in the James River; the eight landing boats of troops in the first stage, where they feinted a landing directly before the American fortified positions; and then the actual point of landing downstream and lines of march toward the American positions.

Petersburg, Va.　25 April 1781

177

SKETCH OF THE SKIRMISH AT PETERSBURG, BETWEEN THE ROYAL ARMY UNDER THE COMMAND OF MAJOR GENL. PHILLIPS AND THE AMERICAN ARMY COMMANDED BY MAJOR GENL. STEWBEN, IN WHICH THE LATTER WERE DEFEATED, APRIL 25TH 1781. BY I. HILLS, LIEUT. 23D REGT. & ASST. ENGR.
London: Wm. Faden, May 3d 1784.
27 x 36 cm.
Scale ca. 1:13,500.
Oriented with north to the left.
Relief shown by hachures.
Includes "references" 1–10.

References. Verner, *Yorktown Campaign* III. Reproduced in *Atlas of the American Revolution*, no. 44.

Variants. A later state, with a ford across the river just to the left of the word "Apamatox," appears in Simcoe's *Journal.* All copies of this later state that have been examined also exhibit two non-plate variations: The words "copied from a plan of Lt. Spencers" have been added in manuscript and the last part of reference seven has been erased.

Copy described. ICN.

Military information. Shows the three-pronged attack of the British under General Phillips with their lines of march and positions of siege. Across the river the American units are deployed (under General Muhlenberg, not Von Steuben as the title suggests).

Osborne's, Va.   27 April 1781

178

SKETCH OF THE ACTION AT OSBURNS, APRIL 27TH 1781. TAKEN ON THE SPOT BY G. SPENCER LT. Q. R.
   [Exeter, 1787]
   18 x 22 cm.
   In John G. Simcoe, *A Journal of the Operations of the Queen's Rangers* (Exeter, Eng., [1787]), opp. p. 140.
   Scale ca. 1:16,250.
   Relief shown by hachures.
   Includes "explanation" A–H.

Reference. Verner, *Yorktown Campaign* VI.

Copy described. ICN.

Military information. Location and lines of fire of the American ships on the James River are indicated, as is the deployment of the several British regiments on the right bank and the American militia on the left.

Spencer's Tavern, Va.   26 June 1781

179

ACTION AT SPENCER'S ORDINARY, JUNE 26TH 1781. TAKEN ON THE SPOT BY G. SPENCER LT. Q.Rs.
   [Exeter, 1787]
   20 x 22 cm.
   In John G. Simcoe, *A Journal of the Operations of the Queen's Rangers* (Exeter, Eng., [1787]), opp. p. 166.
   Scale not indicated.
   Relief shown by hachures.
   Includes references A–N.

Reference. Verner, *Yorktown Campaign* VII.

Copy described. ICN.

Military information. A very detailed plan with troop positions and lines of movement of this comparatively minor engagement.

Chesapeake Capes   5 September 1781

180

A MAP AND CHART OF THOSE PARTS OF THE BAY OF CHESAPEAK, YORK AND JAMES RIVERS, WHICH ARE AT PRESENT THE SEAT OF WAR. JNO. LODGE SC.
London: J. Bew, 30th Novr. 1781.
26 x 38 cm.
In *Political Magazine* 2 (1781): opp. 624.
Scale ca. 1:263,350.
Soundings in fathoms.

References. Verner, *Yorktown Campaign* VIII. Reproduced, in part, in Winsor, *Narrative and Critical History* 6:550.

Copy described. ICN.

Military information. Scanty—shows Cornwallis's entrenchments and "French fleet at anchor Septr. 5th in the morning."

181

CORRECT VIEW OF THE LATE NAVAL ACTION OFF THE CHESAPEAK, WITH OBSERVATIONS. PUBLISHED MONDAY, NOV. 12
[London, November 1781]
12 x 6 cm.
In *Political Magazine* 2 (1781): 620.
Scale ca. 1:450,000.
Oriented with north to the right.
A typographic map, composed entirely with movable type and printers' rule.
Accompanied by a brief textual account.

Reference. An almost identical map is reproduced in Winsor, *Narrative and Critical History* 6:548, where it is attributed to the *London Magazine*. An examination of that periodical failed to reveal the map.

Copy described. ICN.

Military information. A very simplified sketch showing the relative locations of the two fleets.

182

A REPRESENTATION OF THE SEA FIGHT, ON THE 5TH OF SEPR. 1781, BETWEEN REAR ADMIRAL GRAVES AND THE COUNT DE GRASSE
    [London, 1782]
    31 x 39 cm.
    In William Graves, *Two Letters . . . Respecting the Conduct of Rear-Admiral Thomas Graves in North America* ([London, 1782]).
    Scale ca. 1:350,000.
    Includes references A–I, K–O.

References. Verner, *Yorktown Campaign* X. Reproduced in *Atlas of the American Revolution,* no. 45 (2d state).

Variant. A later state, with nineteen additional numbered references and a long "Extract from the Minutes of the General Signals," appears in the *Political Magazine* 6 (1784): opp. 20.

Copy described. ICN.

Military information. Shows the English fleets in five positions, the French in three. Number of ships, guns, and men are shown in a table. The second state identifies the nineteen English ships.

183

SJÖ-BATAILLEN D: 5 SEPT: 1781 UTAN FÖR CHESAPEAKS-BAY K: 5 OM AFTONEN IKAN VINDEN SKRALAL 4 STREK. TAB. II
    [Stockholm, 1787]
    18 x 30 cm.
    In [Carl Gustaf Tornquist], *Grefve Grasses siö-batailler* (Stockholm: Joh. Christ. Holmberg, 1787).
    Scale ca. 1:235,000.

Relief shown by hachures.
Includes references a-g.

Reference. Reproduced in Tornquist, *Naval Campaigns,* p. 175.

Copy described. RPJCB.

Military information. Shows positions of ships and movements of the British and French fleets.

184

POSITION OF THE ENGLISH AND FRENCH FLEETS IMMEDIATELY PREVIOUS TO THE ACTION ON THE 5TH SEPR. 1781. ENGRAVED FOR STEDMANS HISTORY OF THE AMERICAN WAR
  [London, 1794]
  21 x 25 cm.
  In Charles Stedman, *History of the Origin, Progress, and Termination of the American War,* 2 vols. (London: J. Murray, 1794) 2: opp. 400.
  Scale ca. 1:240,000.
  Oriented with north to the upper right.

References. Verner, *Yorktown Campaign* XI. Reproduced in *Magazine of American History* 7 (1881): 369.

Copy described. ICN.

Military information. Shows the mouth of Chesapeake Bay with positions of the ships in the British and French fleets and their lines of movement to the commencement of the engagement.

Rochambeau's March

185

[CÔTE DE YORK-TOWN À BOSTON: MARCHES DE L'ARMÉE. 1782]
  [Paris, 1787]
  27 x 92 cm.
  In François Soulés, *Histoire des troubles de l'Amérique Anglaise,* 4 vols. (Paris: Buisson, 1787) 3: at end.

Scale ca. 1: 1,120,000.
Title from verso of a very similar-appearing manuscript
map in the Rochambeau Collection, Geography and
Map Division, Library of Congress.
Oriented with north toward the upper right.

Reference. Verner, *Yorktown Campaign* XII.

Copy described. ICN.

Military information. Shows sites of fifty-four camps between Williamsburg, Va., and Boston; forty from Providence to Yorktown, Va.; eight from Lebanon, Conn., to near
Philips Burgh, N. Y.; seven between Trenton and Kakiak,
N. J.; and fourteen "marches" from near Annapolis to the
vicinity of Williamsburg. Camps are numbered.

Yorktown, Va.   29 September–18 October 1781

186

A PLAN OF THE ENTRANCE OF CHESAPEAK BAY, WITH JAMES
AND YORK RIVERS; WHEREIN ARE SHEWN THE RESPECTIVE PO-
SITIONS (IN THE BEGINNING OF OCTOBER) 1° OF THE BRITISH
ARMY COMMANDED BY LORD CORNWALLIS, AT GLOUCESTER AND
YORK IN VIRGINIA; 2° OF THE AMERICAN AND FRENCH FORCES
UNDER GENERAL WASHINGTON, 3° AND OF THE FRENCH FLEET
UNDER COUNT DE GRASSE. BY AN OFFICER
London: Wm. Faden, Novr. 26th, 1781.
41 x 52 cm.
Scale ca. 1: 104,600.
Soundings in fathoms.

References. Verner, *Yorktown Campaign* XIV. Reproduced
in *Pennsylvania Magazine of History and Biography* 51
(1927): opp. 193; *Atlas of the American Revolution*, no. 46.

Copy described. MiU-C.

Military information. The title is an adequate summary of
the military information. The situation shown is just before Cornwallis's surrender.

187

PLAN DE L'ARMÉE DE CORNWALLIS ATTAQUÉE ET FAITTE PRISON-
IERE DANS YORK TOWN, LE 19 8BRE PAR L'ARMÉE COMBINÉE
FRANCAISE ET AMERICAINE, DESSINÉ SUR LES LIEUX PAR LES
INGENIEURS DE L'ARMEÉ
  Paris: Le Rouge, Xbre [i.e., December] 1781.
  32 x 40 cm.
  Scale ca. 1:15,000.
  Relief shown by hachures.
  Oriented with north to the upper right.
  Includes "legende" A–G and explanation of colors.
  "Dedié à M. de Vault, Lieutt. Gal. des armées du Roi."
  Dedication covered by blank slip of paper.

References. Reproduced in Library of Congress, *Quarterly
Journal* 30 (1973): 248; *Atlas of the American Revolution,*
no. 47.

Copy described. DLC.

Military information. Very detailed plan of the immediate
Yorktown area with the American, French, and British units
delineated and (in many cases) named. The principal redoubts and batteries are indicated. Shows positions of the
British fleet.

188

BAIE DE CHESAPEAK. PLAN DE L'ATTAQUE DES VILLES DE YORCK
ET GLOUCESTER DANS LESQUELLES ÊTOIT FORTIFIE LE GÉNÉRALE
CORNOWALIS FAIT PRISONNIER, LE 19 OCTOBRE 1781. M. FECIT
  Paris: chez la Ve. de la Gardette Mde. d'estampes [1781?]
  16 x 18 cm.
  Scale ca. 1:75,000.
  Oriented with north to the right.
  Relief shown pictorially and by hachures.
  Includes references A–D.

Reference. Verner, *Yorktown Campaign* XXI.

Copy described. VU.

Military information. American and French camps indicated by clusters of tent symbols; some of the lines are shown, as are ships in the river.

189

To His Excellency Genl. Washington, Commander in Chief of the Armies of the United States of America, this Plan of the Investment of York and Gloucester has been Surveyed and Laid Down, and is Most Humbly Dedicated by His Excellencys Obedient and Very Humble Servant, Sebastn. Bauman, Major of the New York or 2nd Regt of Artillery. This Plan was Taken between the 22nd & 28th of October, 1781. R. Scot sculp.
> Philad[elphia], [February?] 1782.
> 65 x 46 cm.
> Scale ca. 1:14,400.
> Oriented with north toward the upper left.
> Relief shown by hachures.
> Includes "references to the British lines" 1–22 and "explanation" A–R.
> Apparently published in the first quarter of 1782. A prospectus, dated 30 January 1782, states that the map "will shortly be published" (Vietor, *Bauman Map,* p. 16).

References. Stokes and Haskell, pp. 57–58; Verner, *Yorktown Campaign* XXVI; Wheat and Brun 541. Reproduced in *American Heritage Book of the Revolution,* p. 370; *Magazine of American History* 6 (1881): opp. 56; *Atlas of the American Revolution,* no. 48; *Virginia Magazine of History and Biography* 39 (1931): opp. 104; Wheat and Brun, between pp. 124–25.

Copy described. DLC.

Military information. A large, detailed survey done immediately after Cornwallis's capitulation and the first American printed map of the siege and surrender. Shows positions of American and French units (many indicated by name), ships in river, lines of fire from batteries, etc. Successive positions are indicated and keyed to the "explanation"; the "references" detailed number and size of cannon.

190

A PLAN OF THE POSTS OF YORK AND GLOUCESTER IN THE PROVINCE OF VIRGINIA. ESTABLISHED BY HIS MAJESTY'S ARMY UNDER THE COMMAND OF LIEUT. GENERAL EARL CORNWALLIS, TOGETHER WITH THE ATTACKS UNDER OPERATIONS OF THE AMERICAN & FRENCH FORCES COMMANDED BY GENERAL WASHINGTON AND THE COUNT OF ROCHAMBEAU, WHICH TERMINATED IN THE SURRENDER OF THE SAID POSTS AND ARMY ON THE 17TH OF OCTOBER 1781. SURVEYED BY CAPTN. FAGE OF THE ROYAL ARTILLERY

[London: J. F. W. Des Barres] 4th June 1782.

76 x 104 cm.

From J. F. W. Des Barres, *The Atlantic Neptune,* 4 vols. (London, 1774–82).

Scale ca. 1:5,760.

Relief shown by hachures and shading.

With an overlay showing "The position of the army between the ravines on the 28th and 29th of Sept. 1781."

Inset: [Location map of Chesapeake Bay—Hampton Roads—York River area].

References. Henry·N. Stevens, "Catalogue," no. 161; Verner, *Yorktown Campaign* XIII, XV. Reproduced by Barre Publishers, no. 41; in *The Month at Goodspeed's* 29 (1957): 16–17.

Variant. A later state is known, with *chevaux de frise* around British redoubt no. 9 eradicated.

Copy described. MiU-C.

Military information. A careful plan, showing the American and French first and second parallels, fortifications at Gloucester Point and Yorktown, and ships and sunken vessels in the river. British units at Yorktown are identified by number or commander; number and size of cannon are indicated in several British locations.

191

A PLAN OF THE INVESTMENT OF YORK-TOWN AND GLOUCESTER
[Hartford, 1782]
13 x 9 cm.
In Andrew Beers, *The United States Almanack, for the Year 1783* (Hartford: Bavil Webster, [1782]), cover.
Scale ca. 1:63,360.
Oriented with north to the upper left.
On a separate page: "Explanation of the plan" A–I, K–M, O–T, W.
Twenty lettered references appear on the verso.

Reference. Wheat and Brun 542.

Variants. Two variant copies are known, the only differences being in the title, which is set in type. The woodblock itself remains unchanged.

Copy described. MWA.

Military information. A primitive woodcut map. Although the "explanation" locates a number of camps, simply finding the reference letters on the map is difficult.

192

CARTE DU THEATRE DE LA GUERRE PRESENTE EN AMERIQUE. DRESSÉE D'APRÉS LES NOUVELLES CARTES ANGLAISES, PAR L. DENIS
Paris: Basset, 1782.
67 x 50 cm.
Scale ca. 1:5,400,000.
Relief shown pictorially.
Prime meridian: Paris.
Insets: "Plan de l'attaque des villes d'York et de Glocester" (see map 192a)—[Provinces from Massachusetts to New Jersey on a larger scale].
"Dediée et presentée a Monsieur le Noir."

Variant. An earlier state, dated 1779, lacks the York and Gloucester inset.

Copy described. ICN.

Military information. Limited to inset (map 192a).

192a

PLAN DE L'ATTAQUE DES VILLES D'YORK ET DE GLOCESTER SITUÉES EN VIRGINIE, RENDÜES ET LE GÉNÉRAL CORNOWALIS FAIT PRISONIER LE 19. OCTOBRE 1781
[Paris, 1782]
9 x 16 cm.
Inset on map 192.
Scale ca. 1:100,000.
Oriented with north to the bottom.
Relief shown pictorially.

Military information. A small-scale map, very simplified. Shows fortifications around Yorktown; troops and commanders on both sides of river are indicated.

193

CARTE DE LA PARTIE DE LA VIRGINIE OU L'ARMÉE COMBINÉE DE FRANCE & DES ETATS-UNIS DE L'AMÉRIQUE A FAIT PRISONNIERE L'ARMEE ANGLAISE COMMANDÉE PAR LORD CORNWALLIS LE 19 OCTBRE. 1781. AVEC LE PLAN DE L'ATTAQUE D'YORK-TOWN & DE GLOCESTER. LEVÉE ET DESSINÉE SUR LES LIEUX PAR ORDRE DES OFFICIERS GENX. DE L'ARMÉE FRANCAISE & AMERICAINE
Paris: Esnauts et Rapilly [1782?]
47 x 61 cm.
Scale ca. 1:211,400.
Relief shown by hachures.
Prime meridian: Paris.
Served as a source for a map by Brion de la Tour (map 200).

References. Verner, *Yorktown Campaign* XX. Reproduced in *American Heritage Book of the Revolution*, pp. 284–85; Library of Congress, *Quarterly Journal* 30 (1973): 244; *Atlas of the American Revolution*, no. 49.

Variant. A later state is known with the imprint of the publisher Denis added in a circle above the title block.

Copy described. DLC.

Military information. Military units at the sieges of Yorktown and Gloucester are identified by commanders, and the
line of artillery is indicated. The battle lines of the fleets
are shown by symbols for individual ships.

194

Carte générale des colonies Angloises dans l'Amerique
septentrionale pour l'intélligence de la guerre présent.
D'aprés des manuscrits Anglais par J. B. Nolin, géographe.
Corrigée, augmentée des indications des principaux événe-
mens de la guerre avec le tracée des limites pour con-
stituer le traité de paix proposé entre la couronne de la
Grand Bretagne et les Etats Unis. Par R. Philipeau
  Paris: Basset, 1783.
  51 x 72 cm.
  Scale ca. 1:1,700,000.
  Relief shown by hachures.
  Inset: "Suplement qui représente la partie de la Virginie"
  (see map 194a).

Copy described. MiU-C.

Military information. Limited to inset (see map 194a).

194a

Supplément qui représente la partie de la Virginie ou
se trouvent le théâtre ou l'armée combinée des François
et des États Unies a fait prisonnier le Général Cornowalis le 19 Octobre 1781, et le plan d'attaque d'Yorck et
de Glocester par les Generaux Washington et Rochambeau. Le détail de la Baye de Chesapeake. Par L. Denis
  [Paris, 1783]
  28 x 29 cm.
  Inset on map 194.
  Scale ca. 1:2,623,000.
  Includes references 1–12.

Reference. Verner, *Yorktown Campaign* XXII.

Military information. Shows the siege and surrender
through references keyed to rectangular troop symbols.

195

A Plan of York Town and Gloucester in the Province of Virginia, Shewing the Works Constructed for the Defence of those Posts by the British Army under the Command of Lt. Genl. Earl Cornwallis; together with the Attacks and Operations of the American and French Forces Commanded by Genl. Washington and Count Rochambeau, to whom the said Posts were Surrendered on the 17th October 1781. From an Actual Survey in the Possession of Jno. Hills, late Lieut. in the 23rd Regt. & Asst. Engr.

London: Wm. Faden, October 7th 1785.

71 x 54 cm.

Scale ca. 1:5,750.

Relief shown by hachures.

Reference. Verner, *Yorktown Campaign* XVI.

Copy described. ICN.

Military information. Shows fortifications, troop locations, two ships on York River. British troops are identified by name or number of military unit.

196

Plan of the Investment of York & Gloucester by the Allied Armies in Septr. & Octr. 1781

[Trenton, 1785]

22 x 20 cm.

In David Ramsay, *History of the Revolution of South-Carolina*, 2 vols. (Trenton: Isaac Collins, 1785) 2: opp. 326.

Scale ca. 1:29,500.

Oriented with north toward the upper left.

Relief shown by hachures.

Includes "references to the British lines" 1–22.

Served as the source for a map in the French edition of Ramsay (map 199) and for another in Gordon's *History* (map 201).

References. Verner, *Yorktown Campaign* XXVIII; Wheat

and Brun 545. Reproduced in Winsor, *Narrative and Critical History* 6:551.

Copy described. ICN.

Military information. Shows troop positions (French and American units are named), fortifications, ships in river. Number and size of British cannon are given in references.

197

PLAN OF THE SIEGE OF YORK TOWN IN VIRGINIA
   London, March 1st 1787.
   30 x 32 cm.
   In Banastre Tarleton, *History of the Campaigns of 1780 and 1781* (London: T. Cadell, 1787), opp. p. 394.
   Scale ca. 1:18,000.
   Relief shown by hachures.
   Includes two "references" A, B.
   Served as the source for a map in Stedman's *History* (map 202).

Reference. Verner, *Yorktown Campaign* XVII.

Copy described. ICN.

Military information. While on a small scale, this well-engraved map conveys considerable useful information. The ravines and creek beds that figured in the actions are clearly indicated, as are details of the several parallels of the siege. Troop encampments and the artillery park of the Franco-American forces are indicated, and the commanders' names appear. A legend shows the colors used for British, French, and American troops. Lines of fire seaward from the shore batteries appear as do the sunken British vessels and two named ships of the line.

198

PLAN D'YORK EN VIRGINIE, AVEC LES ATTAQUES ET LES CAMPEMENS DE L'ARMÉE COMBINÉE DE FRANCE ET D'AMERIQUE
   [Paris, 1787]
   29 x 39 cm.

In François Soulés, *Histoire des troubles de l'Amérique Anglaise*, 4 vols. (Paris: Buisson, 1787) 3: at end.
Scale ca. 1:24,400.
Oriented with north toward the upper right.
Relief shown by hachures.
Includes references a-d and six-line note.

Reference. Verner, *Yorktown Campaign* XXIII.

Copy described. ICN.

Military information. Shows the British defensive fortifications at Yorktown and Gloucester and the locations of the besieging Franco-American forces as well as the parallels taken up during the attack. The French and American units are named.

199

Plan du siege d'York et de Gloucester par les armées alliées, en Septembre et Octobre 1781. Picquet sculpt.
[Paris, 1787]
22 x 20 cm.
In David Ramsay, *Histoire de la révolution d'Amérique*, 2 vols. (London and Paris, 1787) 2: opp. 398.
Scale ca. 1:50,000.
Oriented with north toward the upper left.
Relief shown by hachures.
Includes "renvois aux lignes Britanniques" 1–22.
Derived directly from a map in the Trenton 1785 edition of Ramsay (map 196).

Reference. Verner, *Yorktown Campaign* XXIV.

Variant. Verner refers to a later state with volume and page numbers in the upper margin.

Copy described. ICN.

Military information. As on map 196.

200

Carte de la partie de la Virginie, ou l'armée combinée de France et des Etats-unis de l'Amérique a fait prisonnière

L'ARMÉE ANGLAISE COMMANDÉE PAR LE LORD CORNWALLIS, LE 19. 8BRE 1781: AVEC LE PLAN D'ATTAQUE D'YORK-TOWN ET DE GLOCESTER. PAR M. BRION DE LA TOUR. GRAVÉ PAR COULUBRIER
Paris: l'auteur [1787?]
22 x 31 cm.
Scale ca. 1:256,000.
Prime meridians: Paris and Ferro.
Includes "renvois" A–I, K–L.
"Prix 12 s."
Based, in part, on the Esnauts et Rapilly map (map 193).

Reference. Verner, *Yorktown Campaign* XXV.

Copy described. ViHi.

Military information. Shows troop locations at Yorktown and Glouce'ster, ships in river, arc of ships in Chesapeake Bay. Some of the French corps are named.

201

YORK TOWN AND GLOUCESTER POINT, AS BESIEGED BY THE ALLIED ARMY. ENGRAVED FOR DR. GORDON'S HISTORY OF THE AMERICAN WAR. T. CONDER SCULPT.
London [1788]
29 x 22 cm.
In William Gordon, *History of the Rise, Progress, and Establishment of the Independence of the United States,* 4 vols. (London, 1788) 4: opp. 196.
Scale ca. 1:32,000.
Oriented with north towards the upper left.
Relief shown by hachures.
Includes "explanation" 1–22, B–R and note.
Derived from a map in Ramsay's *History* (map 196).

Reference. Verner, *Yorktown Campaign* XVIII.

Copy described. ICN.

Military information. As on map 196.

202

PLAN OF THE SIEGE OF YORK TOWN IN VIRGINIA. ENGRAVED FOR STEDMANS HISTORY OF THE AMERICAN WAR

[London, 1794]

28 x 33 cm.

In Charles Stedman, *History of the Origin, Progress, and Termination of the American War,* 2 vols. (London: J. Murray, 1794) 2: opp. 412.

Scale ca. 1:18,000.

Relief shown by hachures.

Includes "references" A, B.

Derived from the map in Tarleton's *History* (map 197). Served as the source for a map in the German edition of Stedman (map 203).

References. Verner, *Yorktown Campaign* XIX. Reproduced in *Magazine of American History* 6 (1881): opp. 8.

Copy described. ICN.

Military information. As on map 197, but the legend identifying the troops of the three nations involved uses symbols rather than colors.

203

PLAN DER BELAGERUNG VON YORK-TOWN IN VIRGINIA. ZU STEDMANS GESCHICHTE DES AMERIKANISCHEN KRIEGES. D. E. SOTZMANN DEL. A. SANDER FECIT.

[Berlin, 1795]

14 x 16 cm.

In Charles Stedman, *Geschichte des Ursprungs, des Fortgangs, und der Beendigung des amerikanischen Kriegs,* 2 vols. (Berlin: Voss, 1795) 2.

Scale ca. 1:39,500.

Relief shown by hachures.

Derived from the map in the English edition (map 202).

Reference. Verner, *Yorktown Campaign* XXX.

Copy described. RPJCB.

Military information. As on map 202.

7

EUROPEAN ENGAGEMENTS

Gibraltar Siege   6 July 1779–6 February 1783

204

A Plan of the Town and Fortifications of Gibraltar with the Spanish Lines &c.
London: Robt. Sayer & Jno. Bennett, 27 Novr. 1779.
35 x 52 cm.
Scale ca. 1:14,200.
Oriented with north to the left.
Relief shown pictorially and by hachures.
Includes "references" A–I, K–S.
Insets: "A Chart of the Straits of Gibraltar"—[The Bay of Gibraltar].
The British Museum *Catalogue* lists later states published in 1782 and 1787.

Copy described. BL.

Military information. Shows batteries (keyed to "references"), Spanish lines, etc. On the isthmus are shown "batteries of the besiegers raised in October 1779."

205

A Plan of the Town and Fortifications of Gibraltar, with the New Works Made (since the Last Siege) for Its Better Security; also the Lines the Spaniards have Erected in Their Present Operations against that Place
London: Robert Wilkinson, 1st Jany. 1780.
22 x 69 cm.
Scale ca. 1:12,000.
Oriented with north toward the left.

Relief shown pictorially; soundings in fathoms.

Includes "references" A–C, 1–40.

Apparently the source for a map in the *Political Magazine* (map 206).

Copy described. BL.

Military information. Shows lines, batteries, and fortifications. The references are mostly to military positions and describe their function in previous sieges. A note states that "the old approaches [are] coloured yellow, the present approaches [are] cold. blue."

206

A PLAN OF THE TOWN AND FORTIFICATIONS OF GIBRALTAR. JN. LODGE SCULP.

[London, January 1780]

13 x 29 cm.

In *Political Magazine* 1 (1780): opp. 35.

Scale ca. 1:25,700.

Oriented with north to the left.

Relief shown pictorially.

Pages 34 and 35 have "references to the plan of Gibraltar" 1–40.

Apparently derived from the Wilkinson map (map 205). Served as the source for a map published in Dublin (map 207).

Copy described. ICN.

Military information. As on map 205, except that this map does not show the "new approaches."

207

A PLAN OF THE TOWN AND FORTIFICATIONS OF GIBRALTAR

[Dublin, February 1780]

13 x 29 cm.

In *Walker's Hibernian Magazine* (1780): opp. 65.

Scale ca. 1:26,000.

Oriented with north to the left.

Relief shown pictorially, soundings in fathoms.

"References to the plan of Gibraltar" 1–40, appear on pp. 154–55.

Derived directly from a map in the *Political Magazine* (map 206).

Copy described. ICN.

Military information. As on map 206.

208

A PLAN OF THE ATTACK MADE NOVBER. 27TH 1781 BY A DE-TACHMENT COMMANDED BY BRIGADIER-GENERAL ROSS, FROM THE GARRISON OF GIBRALTAR, ON THE ENEMY'S WORKS ERECTED BEFORE THAT FORTRESS

London: Engraved and published by Wm. Faden, March 25th 1782.

60 x 45 cm.

Scale ca. 1:3,900.

Relief shown by hachures.

Includes "references" A–D.

Inset: "Ordre de bataille of the detachment for the sortie" [organizational diagram].

Dedication: "To His Excellency . . . George Augustus Elliott . . . by John Drinkwater."

Very similar to a plan published in 1785 (map 214); both probably based on the same prototype.

Copy described. BL.

Military information. A very detailed plan showing units to the regimental level, lines of march, fortifications, etc. Commanders' names are indicated in the inset diagram. The map is centered on "the neutral ground" between the Rock of Gibraltar and the Spanish lines.

209

PROSPECT VON DER GEBERIGIGTEN HAUPT VESTUNG GIBRALTAR UND DESSEN DABEŸ HERUM LIEGENDEN GEGENDEN, SO WIE DIESELBE SICH BËY DER IETZIGEN BEGEBENHEIT BEFINDET, DURCH EIN EINGESCHICKTES BROLLONG IST SOLCHES IN EIN RICHTIGES ORGINAL DARGESTELLET UND BEZEICHNET, SO WIE

AUCH DIESE STARKE VESTUNG DURCH NEUE ANLAGEN DER VESTUNGS WERCKE VON DEN ENGLÄNDERN BALD UNÜBERWIND- LICH GEMACHT INDEM DIESELBE SCHON A 1705 VON 30 000 FRANZOSEN UND SPANIERR BELAGERT, GEGEN 1200 ENGLISCHER GARNISON MIT GROSSEM VERLUST HABEN ABZIEHEN MÜSSEN, DIESES ALLES WIRD IN BEISTEHENDER EXPLICATION DEUTLICH ANGEWIESEN. J. J. RAMBERGER, ARC. J. HILBERS, SCULP.
[Augsburg?] 1782.
40 x 75 cm.
Scale ca. 1:14,300.
Oriented with north to the upper left (not to the left as indicated by north arrow).
Relief shown pictorially and by hachures.
Includes two columns of letterpress "erktärung" 1–52, signed "J. J. R. Archit."

Copy described. BL.

Military information. Lines, land batteries, ships, and the floating batteries are shown in this primitive engraving that is half-map and half-view. Many explanations refer to the siege of September-October 1782.

210

PLAN DE GIBRALTAR, ATTAQUÉ PAR TERRE ET PAR MER PAR L'ARMÉE ESPAGNOLE ET FRANÇAISE AUX ORDRES DE MR. LE DUC DE CRILLON, EN PRESÉNCE DE MGR. LE COMPTE D'ARTOIS. D'APRÈS LES DESSINS D'UN INGÉNIEUR EN CHEF DE L'ARMÉE. CHAULMIER SCULP.
Paris: Esnauts et Rapilly, 1782.
75 x 52 cm.
Scale ca. 1:82,350.
Relief shown pictorially and by hachures; soundings in fathoms.
Prime meridian: Ferro.
Shows only the Bay of Gibraltar.
Inset: [Peninsula of Gibraltar] (see map 210a).

Reference. Reproduced in *Atlas of the American Revolution*, no. 50.

Copy described. ICN.

Military information. Shows ships firing on city, tents of encampment at north end of bay.

210a

[PENINSULA OF GIBRALTAR]
  [Paris, 1782]
  74 x 26 cm.
  Inset on map 210.
  Scale ca. 1:8,600.
  Relief shown pictorially and by hachures; soundings in fathoms.

Military information. A large-scale, detailed plan showing lines, batteries, works, encampments, magazines, etc., on the mainland. Ships and floating batteries are shown on the bay with the lines of their fire prominently indicated.

211

PLAN OF THE BAY, ROCK, AND TOWN OF GIBRALTAR, FROM AN ACTUAL SURVEY BY AN OFFICER WHO WAS AT GIBRALTAR FROM 1769 TO 1775, WITH THE WORKS, BATTERIES, AND INCAMPMENT OF THE SPANISH ARMY ON THE 19TH OF OCTOR. 1782, THE POSITION OF THE COMBINED FLEET, AND THE ATTACK BY THE BATTERING SHIPS SEPTR. 13TH OF THE SAME YEAR. ENGRAVED BY WILLIAM FADEN
  London: William Faden, Jany. 26th 1783.
  51 x 71 cm.
  Scale ca. 1:25,000.
  Oriented with north to the right.
  Relief shown by hachures; soundings in fathoms.
  Very similar to a map published in 1786 (map 215); both probably based on the same prototype.

Copy described. BL.

Military information. A detailed, careful plan showing the siege of 1782. Troop positions, batteries, lines, and artillery parks are indicated on land. The naval action is indicated by battering ships before Gibraltar and Algeciras, fire ships, "a boom," bridges of boats, etc.

212

[PENINSULA OF GIBRALTAR]
  [Venice, 1783]
  12 x 32 cm. on sheet 26 x 36 cm.
  In [Paul U. Dubuisson], *Storia della rivoluzione dell'*
    America inglese, 3 vols. (Venice: Vincenzio Formaleoni,
    1782–84) 2: opp. 81.
  Scale ca. 1:25,000.
  Oriented with north toward the left.
  Relief shown pictorially.
  Includes references 1–14.
  Inset: [Port Mahon, Minorca, including Fort San Filippo]

Copy described. ICN.

Military information. Shows fortifications, batteries, English and Spanish camps.

213

A PLAN OF THE BATTERIES ERECTED BEFORE GIBRALTAR, WITH THE ATTACKS MADE BY SEA AND LAND ON THAT GARRISON BY THE DUKE DE CRILLON AND ADMIRAL MORENO ON THE 13TH OF SEPTEMBER, 1782, IN PRESENCE OF THE COMBINED FLEETS OF FRANCE AND SPAIN. D. 72D REGT. DELINT. ASHBY SCULP.
  [London], Augst. 16th 1785.
  47 x 33 cm.
  In John Drinkwater Bethune, *A History of the Late Siege*
    of Gibraltar (London: T. Spilsbury, 1786), opp. p. 294.
  Scale ca. 1:7,350.
  Oriented with north toward the upper left.
  Relief shown by hachures.
  Includes "sections of a Spanish magazine and splinter
    proof" and, on page 294, "reference to the plan of the
    grand attack" 1–44.
  Inset view: "Larboard & starboard sides of a battering
    ship."

Reference. A manuscript version of this plan, possibly the engraver's copy, is reproduced in Library of Congress, *Quarterly Journal* 30 (1973): 260.

Copy described. ICN.

Military information. A detailed plan. "Battering ships" are shown in the bay, and many land batteries are located.

214

A Plan Shewing the Attack and Disposition of the Detachment which Sallied on the 27th of Novemr. 1781 from Gibraltar and Destroyed the Spanish Batteries before that Garrison. D: 72 Regt. delint. J. Cheevers sculpt.

[London], Augst. 16th 1785.

47 x 34 cm.

In John Drinkwater Bethune, *A History of the Late Siege of Gibraltar* (London: T. Spilsbury, 1786), opp. p. 204.

Scale ca. 1:6,070.

Oriented with north toward the upper left.

Relief shown by hachures and shading.

Inset: "The detachment formed for the sortie" [organizational diagram].

Pages 203–4 include "references to the plan of the sortie" A–I, K–T, V–Z.

Very similar to a map published in 1782 (map 208); both probably based on the same prototype.

Copy described. ICN.

Military information. As on map 208.

215

A Chart of the Bay of Gibraltar, Including a Small Plan of that Fortress, with the Position of the Military & Naval Force of France and Spain Present during the Late Siege of that Garrison. J. Cheevers sculpt.

[London, 1786]

46 x 67 cm.

In John Drinkwater Bethune, *A History of the Late Siege of Gibraltar* (London: T. Spilsbury, 1786), opp. p. 46.

Scale ca. 1:25,000.

Oriented with north to the right.

Relief shown by hachures and shading.

Includes "reference" A–G; "garrison [refs.]" 1–22.

Very similar to a map published in 1783 (map 211); both probably based on the same prototype.

Copy described. ICN.

Military information. As on map 211.

"Bonhomme Richard"–"Serapis" Engagement
23 September 1779

216

[ACTION BETWEEN THE BONHOMME RICHARD, THE SERAPIS, AND THE ALLIANCE, SEPTEMBER 1779]
    [Boston, 1784]
    14 maps, sizes vary from 2 x 5 cm. to 9 x 12 cm.
    In Pierre Landais, *Memorial, to Justify Peter Landai's Conduct during the Late War* (Boston: Peter Edes, 1784), pp. 37–43.
    Scales vary.

Reference. Wheat and Brun 743.

Copy described. MiU-C.

Military information. This series of plans shows ship positions during various phases of the naval engagement off Flamborough Head.

Port Praia, Cape Verde Islands   16 April 1781

217

A MAP OF THE CAPE DE VERD ISLANDS, WITH THE ADJACENT COAST OF AFRICA, THE SETTLEMENTS OF SENEGAL, GAMBIA AND GOREE, ALSO A PLAN OF PORT PRAYA IN ST. JAGO. JNO. LODGE SCULP.
    London, J. Bew, 30th June 1781.
    22 x 43 cm.
    In *Political Magazine* 2 (1781): opp. 386.
    Scale ca. 1:2,750,000.
    Relief shown pictorially and by hachures; soundings in fathoms.
    Inset: "A Correct Plan of Port Praya" (see map 217a).

Copy described. ICN.

Military information. Limited to inset (see map 217a).

217a

A Correct Plan of Port Praya, in the South Part of St. Jago, where the French Fleet Attacked Commodore Johnstone
[London, 30 June 1781]
10 x 16 cm.
Inset on map 217.
Scale ca. 1:51,700.
Soundings in fathoms.

Military information. Shows positions of seventeen ships in the bay; thirteen are named.

218

Station of the Ships in Port Praya Bay when the Engagement began between Come. Johnstone & M. de Suffrien. Gent. Mag. Supt.
[London, January 1782]
16 x 26 cm.
In *Gentleman's Magazine* 51 (1781, Supplement): opp. 617.
Scale not indicated.
In upper right corner: Fig. 1 [silhouette of a head].

Copy described. ICN.

Military information. British fleet depicted in the harbor and named; French fleet named and number of cannon and details of the engagement are indicated. A long letter describing the action occupies eight columns of accompanying text in the magazine.

REFERENCES

This list includes 1) contemporary publications containing military maps, 2) cartobibliographies consulted, and 3) works cited in the descriptions. Numbers following entries for contemporary works refer to individual maps in this bibliography, not pages.

Adams, Randolph Greenfield. *British Headquarters Maps and Sketches Used by Sir Henry Clinton while in Command of the British Forces Operating in North America during the War for Independence, 1775–1782: A Descriptive List of the Original Manuscripts and Printed Documents now Preserved in the William L. Clements Library at the University of Michigan.* Ann Arbor: William L. Clements Library, 1928.

———. "The Cartography of the British Attack on Fort Moultrie in 1776." In *Essays Offered to Herbert Putnam,* edited by William Warner Bishop and Andrew Keogh, pp. 35–46. New Haven: Yale University Press, 1929.

Almon, John. See *The Remembrancer*

The American Campaigns of Rochambeau's Army 1780, 1781, 1782, 1783. Translated and edited by Howard C. Rice, Jr., and Anne S. K. Brown. 2 vols. Princeton, N. J.: Princeton University Press; Providence, R. I.: Brown University Press, 1972.

The American Heritage Book of the Revolution. Editor-in-charge, Richard M. Ketchum. New York: American Heritage Publishing Co. [1958].

[Anburey, Thomas]. *Travels Through the Interior Parts of America, In a Series of Letters by an Officer.* 2 vols. London: William Lane, 1789.   59

Atlas of the American Revolution. Map selection and commentary by Kenneth Nebenzahl; narrative text by Don Higginbotham. Chicago: Rand McNally, 1974.

Barre Publishers. *See* Des Barres, J. F. W.

Beers, Andrew. *The United-States Almanack, for the Year of our Lord Christ, 1783.* Hartford: Bavil Webster [1782]. 191

Begnaud, Allen Eustis. "British Operations in the Caribbean and the American Revolution." Ph.D. dissertation, Tulane University, 1966.

Bethune, John Drinkwater. *A History of the Late Siege of Gibraltar; with a Description and Account of that Garrison; from the Earliest Periods.* London: T. Spilsbury, 1786. 213, 214, 215

Boatner, Mark Mayo. *Encyclopedia of the American Revolution.* New York: D. McKay Co. [1966].

Boston. Engineering Dept. *List of Maps of Boston Published between 1614 and 1822, Copies of Which are to be Found in the Possession of the City of Boston or other Collectors of the Same.* Boston: Municipal Printing Office, 1902.

British Museum. *Catalogue of Printed Maps, Charts, and Plans.* Photolithographic ed. 15 vols. London: Trustees of the British Museum, 1967.

Burgoyne, John. *A State of the Expedition from Canada, as Laid before the House of Commons . . . and Verified by Evidence; with a Collection of Authentic Documents.* London: J. Almon, 1780. 48, 51, 52, 53, 56, 57

———. *A Supplement to the State of the Expedition from Canada, Containing General Burgoyne's Orders, Respecting the Principal Movements and Operations of the Army to the Raising of the Siege of Ticonderoga.* London: J. Robson, 1780. 49

Calef, John. *The Siege of Penobscot by the Rebels.* London: G. Kearsley, 1781. 39

Canada, Public Archives of. [Catalog of the "Atlantic Neptune" collection, Public Archives of Canada. Ottawa, 196–]. Xeroxed.

Carter, William. *A Genuine Detail of the Several Engagements, Positions, and Movements of the Royal and American Armies, during the Years 1775 and 1776.* London: G. Kearsley, 1784. 33

Cartografia de Ultramar. 4 vols. and 4 atlases. Madrid: Imprenta del Servicio Geográfico del Ejército, 1949–57.

Chapin, Howard Millar. *Check List of Maps of Rhode Island.* Contributions to Rhode Island Bibliography, no. 5. Providence: Preston & Rounds Co., 1918.

Clark, David Sanders. *Index to Maps of the American Revolution in Books and Periodicals Illustrating the Revolutionary War and Other Events of the Period 1763–1789.* Washington, D. C., 1969.

Cobb, David Allan. *Vermont Maps Prior to 1900: An Annotated Cartobibliography.* Vermont History, vol. 39, nos. 3 & 4. Montpelier: Vermont Historical Society, 1971.

Cumming, William Patterson. *The Southeast in Early Maps, with an Annotated Check List of Printed and Manuscript Regional and Local Maps of Southeastern North America During the Colonial Period.* [2d ed.] Chapel Hill: University of North Carolina Press [1962].

[Daboll, Nathan]. *Freebetter's New-England Almanack, for the Year of Our Lord Christ 1777.* Hartford: N. Patten [1776].   97

Des Barres, Joseph Frederick Wallet. *The Atlantic Neptune.* 4 vols. London, 1774–82; facsimile reprint, Barre, Mass.: Barre Publishers, 1966–69. Of six projected portfolios in the Barre facsimile, only the first four have been completed.   3, 31, 36, 54, 75, 79, 80, 89, 99, 136, 190

[Driver, Clive E.] *Early American Maps and Views.* Philadelphia: The Philip H. & A. S. W. Rosenbach Foundation, 1972.

[Dubuisson, Paul Ulric]. *Storia della rivoluzione dell' America inglese.* 3 vols. Venice: Vincenzio Formaleoni, 1782–84.   212

European Magazine and London Review. London: J. Fielding et al., 1782–1823.   160

Evans, Charles. *American Bibliography.* 14 vols. Chicago, 1903–59.

Evans, Geraint N. D. *Uncommon Obdurate: The Several Public Careers of J. F. W. Des Barres.* Salem, Mass.: Peabody Museum, 1969.

Faden, William. *Atlas of Battles of the American Revolution, together with Maps Shewing the Routes of the British and American Armies, Plans of Cities, Surveys of Harbors, &c., Taken during That Eventful Period by Officers Attached to the Royal Army.* [New York: Bartlett & Welford, 1845?]

———. *A Catalogue of Maps, Charts, and Plans.* [London], 1778.

———. *Catalogue of the Geographical Works, Maps, Plans,*

&c. *Published by W. Faden.* [London], 1822; reprinted [London]: Map Collectors' Circle [1963].

———. *The North American Atlas, Selected from the Most Authentic Maps, Charts, Plans, &c. hitherto Published.* London, 1777.   34, 35, 43, 44, 47, 64, 101, 116, 119, 130

Fite, Emerson D., and Freeman, Archibald. *A Book of Old Maps Delineating American History from the Earliest Days Down to the Close of the Revolutionary War.* Cambridge, Mass.: Harvard University Press, 1926; reprinted New York: Dover, 1969; Arno Press, 1969.

Frothingham, Richard. *History of the Siege of Boston, and of the Battles of Lexington, Concord, and Bunker Hill.* 2d ed. Boston: Charles C. Little and James Brown, 1851.

Galloway, Joseph. *Letters to a Nobleman, on the Conduct of the War in the Middle Colonies.* London: J. Wilkie, 1779.   124

General Magazine; or, Compleat Repository of Arts, Sciences, Politics and Literature. London: G. Allen, 1776–77.   17

Gentleman's and London Magazine; or, Monthly Chronologer. Dublin: John Exshaw, 1741–94.   120

The Gentleman's Magazine. London: F. Jefferies et al., 1731–1907.   27, 100, 148, 218

Geographische Belustigungen zur Erläuterung der neuesten Weltgeschichte. Stück 1. Leipzig: J. C. Müller, 1776.   19

Georgia Historical Society. *Collections.* Savannah, 1840–1916.

Gordon, William. *The History of the Rise, Progress, and Establishment of the Independence of the United States of America.* 4 vols. London, 1788.   23, 63, 86, 105, 201

Grasse-Tilly, François Joseph Paul, marquis de. *Mémoire du Comte de Grasse, sur le combat naval du 12 avril 1782, avec les plans des positions principales des armées respectives.* [Paris, 1782]; photostat reproduction [Boston: Massachusetts Historical Society, 1928].   164

———. *Memorie van den Graave de Grasse, betreffende de actien in de West-Indiën voorgevallen.* [Amsterdam, 1782].   165

Graves, William. *Two Letters from W. Graves, Esq., Respecting the Conduct of Rear-Admiral Thomas Graves, in North America, during His Accidental Command There for Four Months in 1781.* [London, 1782].   182

Green, Samuel Abbott. *Ten Fac-simile Reproductions Relating to New England.* Boston, 1902.

Guthorn, Peter Jay. *American Maps and Map Makers of the Revolution.* Monmouth Beach, N. J.: Philip Freneau Press, 1966.

————. *British Maps of the American Revolution.* Monmouth Beach, N. J.: Philip Freneau Press, 1972.

[Hall, John]. *The History of the Civil War in America, Vol. I. Comprehending the Campaigns of 1775, 1776 and 1777.* London: T. Payne, 1780.   103

Haskell, Daniel Carl. *Manhattan Maps: A Co-operative List.* New York: The New York Public Library, 1931. "Reprinted from the Bulletin of the New York Public Library of April–May & July–October 1930."

Henry E. Huntington Library & Art Gallery. *See* Museum Book Store

Hilliard d'Auberteuil, Michel René. *Essais historiques et politiques sur les Anglo-Américains.* 2 vols. Brussels, 1781–82.   140

Historic Urban Plans. Historic City Plans and Views. Ithaca, N. Y., 1965–. [Series of facsimile reproductions.]

Howes, Wright. *U. S. Iana (1650–1950): A Selective Bibliography in Which are Described 11,620 Uncommon and Significant Books Relating to the Continental Portion of the United States.* Rev. ed. New York: R. R. Bowker, for The Newberry Library, 1962.

Hutchins, John Nathan. *Hutchin's Improved: Being an Almanack and Ephemeris . . . for the Year of Our Lord 1776.* New York: Hugh Gaine, [1775].   9

Jefferys, Thomas. *The American Atlas: or, a Geographical Description of the Whole Continent of America.* London: R. Sayer and J. Bennett, 1778.   46

Karpinski, Louis C., and Smith, Priscilla. *Early Maps of Carolina and Adjoining Regions from the Collection of Henry P. Kendall.* 2d ed. Charleston, S. C.: Carolina Art Association, 1937.

Klein, Christopher Miller. *Maps in Eighteenth-Century British Magazines.* Forthcoming.

[Korn, Christoph Heinrich]. *Geschichte der Kriege in und ausser Europa.* 30 pts. [Nuremberg]: Gabriel Nicolaus Raspe, 1776–84.   102, 117, 134

Landais, Pierre. *Memorial, to Justify Peter Landai's Conduct during the Late War.* Boston: Peter Edes, 1784.   216

Laney, Francis Baker, and Wood, Katharine Hill. "List of Maps of North Carolina." In *Bibliography of North Carolina Geology, Mineralogy and Geography*, pp. 270–362. North Carolina Geological and Economic Survey, Bulletin no. 18. Raleigh: E. M. Uzzell & Co., 1909.

Le Rouge, George Louis. *Atlas Ameriquain septentrional*. Paris, 1778.   67, 135

———. *Pilote Americain septentrional*. Paris, 1778.   37

Lee, John Thomas. "Captain Jonathan Carver: Additional Data." In Wisconsin State Historical Society, *Proceedings* (1912), pp. 87–123.

Library of Congress. *Quarterly Journal*. Washington, 1943–.

Lindsay, Colin. *Extracts from Colonel Tempelhoffe's History of the Seven Years War. . . to Which is Added a Narrative of Events at St. Lucie and Gibraltar, and of John Duke of Marlborough's March to the Danube*. 2 vols. London: T. Cadell, 1793.   150

Lingel, Robert. "The Atlantic Neptune." In *Bulletin of the New York Public Library* 40 (1936): 571–603.

London Magazine; or, Gentleman's Monthly Intelligencer. London: J. Wilford et al., 1732–85.   42, 115

Low, Nathaniel. *An Astronomical Diary; or, Almanack for the Year of Christian Aera, 1777*. Boston: J. Gill, [1776].   96

Lowery, Woodbury. *The Lowery Collection: A Descriptive List of Maps of the Spanish Possessions within the Present Limits of the United States, 1502–1820*. Edited with notes by Philip Lee Phillips. Washington: G. P. O., 1912.

McCormack, Helen G. "A Catalogue of Maps of Charleston Based on the Collection of Engraved and Photostatic Copies Owned by Alfred O. Halsey." In *Year Book: City of Charleston, S. C., 1944*, pp. 179–202. Charleston: City Council, 1947.

Magazine of American History, with Notes and Queries. New York & Chicago: A. S. Barnes & Co., 1877–93.

Massachusetts Historical Society. Americana Series; Photostat Reproductions by the Massachusetts Historical Society. No. 211. *See* Grasse-Tilly, *Mémoire*

Mathews, Edward B. "Cartography." In *Bibliography and Cartography of Maryland*, pp. 332–401. Maryland Geological Survey, Special Publication, vol. 1, pt. 4. Baltimore: Johns Hopkins Press, 1897.

[Matthews, John]. *Korte verklaringe van verscheidene ac-*

tiën, tusschen de Engelsche en Fransche vlooten, gedu-urende den laasten oorlog in de West-Indiën voorgevallen. Amsterdam: Gerard Hulst van Keulen, 1791.   153, 155, 159, 163, 173, 174

———. *Twenty-one Plans, with Explanations, of Different Actions in the West Indies, during the Late War.* Chester: J. Fletcher, 1784.   152, 154, 157, 161, 166, 167

Michigan, University of, William L. Clements Library. *British Maps of the American Revolution: A Guide to an Exhibit in the William L. Clements Library.* Ann Arbor, 1936.

———. *Research Catalog of Maps of America to 1860.* Edited by Douglas W. Marshall. 4 vols. Boston: G. K. Hall, 1972.

The Month at Goodspeed's. Boston: Goodspeed's, 1929–69.

Murray, James. *An Impartial History of the Present War in America.* 3 vols. Newcastle upon Tyne: T. Robson [1778–80].   30

———. *An Impartial History of the War in America.* 3 vols. Boston: Nathaniel Coverly and Robert Hodge, 1781–84.   32

Museum Book Store. *A Catalogue of Maps of America from the Middle of the Sixteenth to the Middle of the Nineteenth Centuries.* No. 93. London, 1924. [All items in the Huntington Library.]

———. *Catalogue of Rare Maps of America.* No. 110. London, 1928.

———. *A Catalogue of Rare Maps of America from the Sixteenth to Nineteenth Centuries.* No. 105. London, 1927. [All items in the Huntington Library.]

The New-York and Country Almanack for the Year 1776. New York: Shober and Loudon [1775].   10

New York Public Library. *Dictionary Catalog of the Map Division.* 10 vols. Boston: G. K. Hall, 1971.

New York State Library. *Catalogue of Maps and Surveys in the Offices of the Secretary of State, of the State Engineer and Surveyor, and in the New York State Library.* Albany: Weed, Parsons and Co., 1851.

North American City Plans. Map Collectors' Series, no. 20. London: Map Collectors' Circle, 1965.

The North American Pilot for Newfoundland, Labradore, the Gulf and River St. Laurence; being a Collection of Sixty Accurate Charts and Plans, Drawn from Original Surveys . . . Chiefly Engraved by the Late Thomas Jefferys. 2 vols. London: R. Sayer and J. Bennett, 1778–79.   65

[O'Beirne, Thomas L.], *A Candid and Impartial Narrative of the Transactions of the Fleet under the Command of Lord Howe, from the Arrival of the Toulon Squadron, on the Coast of America, to the Time of His Lordship's Departure for England.* 2d ed. London: J. Almon [1779]. 141

Pennsylvania Magazine of History and Biography. Philadelphia: The Historical Society of Pennsylvania, 1877–.

The Pennsylvania Magazine; or, American Monthly Museum. 2 vols. Philadelphia: R. Aitken, [1775–76]. 2, 5

Phillips, Philip Lee, comp. *A List of Geographical Atlases in the Library of Congress with Bibliographical Notes.* 7 vols. Washington: G. P. O., 1909–. (Vols. 5–7 comp. by Clara Egli LeGear.) Vols. 1–4 reprinted Amsterdam: Theatrum Orbis Terrarum [1967?].

———. *A List of Maps of America in the Library of Congress preceded by a List of Works Relating to Cartography.* Washington: G. P. O., 1901; reprints New York: Burt Franklin, 1967; Amsterdam: Theatrum Orbis Terrarum, 1967.

———. *Virginia Cartography: A Bibliographical Description.* Smithsonian Miscellaneous Collections 1039, vol. 39. Washington: Smithsonian Institution, 1896.

The Political Magazine and Parliamentary, Naval, Military, and Literary Journal. London: J. Bew, 1780–91. 70, 88, 104, 156, 180, 181, 182, 206, 217

Ramsay, David. *Histoire de la révolution d'Amérique par rapport a la Caroline Méridionale.* 2 vols. London and Paris: Froullé, 1787. 62, 73, 84, 85, 199

———. *The History of the Revolution of South-Carolina, from a British Province to an Independent State.* 2 vols. Trenton, N. J.: Isaac Collins, 1785. 61, 72, 81, 82, 196

Rapin-Thoyras, Paul de. *Rapin's Impartial History of England . . . with the Continuation to the Year 1786.* 5 vols. London: J. Harrison, 1784–89. 40

The Remembrancer; or, Impartial Repository of Public Events. 17 vols. London: J. Almon, 1775–84. 4

Ristow, Walter William. "Cartography of the Battle of Bunker Hill." Paper read at Fifth International Conference on the History of Cartography, Edinburgh, 23 September 1971. Mimeographed.

———. *Guide to the History of Cartography: An Annotated*

List of References on the History of Maps and Mapmaking. Washington: Library of Congress, 1973.

————. "Maps of the American Revolution: A Preliminary Survey." In Library of Congress, *Quarterly Journal* 28 (1971): 196–215.

————, and Graziani, Mary E. *Facsimiles of Rare Historical Maps: A List of Reproductions for Sale by Various Publishers and Distributors.* 3d ed. Washington: Library of Congress, 1968; supplement, 1971.

Rivington's New-York Gazetter; or, the Connecticut, Hudson's River, New-Jersey, and Quebec Weekly Advertiser. 3 August 1775.   25

Sabin, Joseph. *Bibliotheca Americana: A Dictionary of Books Relating to America from Its Discovery to the Present Time. Begun by Joseph Sabin and Continued by Wilberforce Eames for the Bibliographical Society of America.* 29 vols. New York, 1868–1936.

St. Clair, Arthur. *Proceedings of a General Court Martial, held at White Plains, in the State of New-York . . . for the Trial of Maj. Gen. St. Clair, August 25, 1778.* Philadelphia: Hall and Sellers, 1778.   50

Sayer, Robert, and Bennett, John. *The American Military Pocket Atlas; being an Approved Collection of Correct Maps, both General and Particular, of the British Colonies; Especially Those Which now are, or Probably may be, the Theatre of War.* London [1776].   41, 46

The Scots Magazine. Edinburgh: Sands, Brymer, Murray and Cochran et al., 1739–1825.   26

Simcoe, John Graves. *A Journal of the Operations of the Queen's Rangers, from the End of the Year 1777 to the Conclusion of the Late American War.* Exeter, [1787].   137, 138, 142, 143, 144, 175, 176, 177, 178, 179

————. *Simcoe's Military Journal: A History of the Operations of a Partisan Corps called the Queen's Rangers.* New York: Bartlett & Welford, 1844.

Soulés, François. *Histoire des troubles de l'Amérique Anglaise, ecrite sur les mémoires les plus authentiques.* 4 vols. Paris: Buisson, 1787.   185, 198

Stearns, Samuel. *The North American's Almanack, for the Year of Our Lord, 1777.* Worcester: Stearns and Bigelow [1776].   98

Stedman, Charles. *Geschichte des Ursprungs, des Fortgangs, und der Beendigung des amerikanischen Kriegs.* 2 vols.

Berlin: Voss, 1795.   58, 106, 203

————. *The History of the Origin, Progress, and Termination of the American War.* 2 vols. London: J. Murray, 1794.   29, 55, 57, 76, 87, 90, 91, 92, 93, 101, 113, 116, 139, 184, 202

Stevens, Henry Newton. "Catalogue of the Henry Newton Stevens Collection of the Atlantic Neptune, together with a Concise Bibliographical Description of Every Chart, View, and Leaf of Text Contained therein, as also of Certain Other States Observed Elsewhere." Corrected, revised & augmented by Henry Stevens. London: Henry Stevens, Son & Stiles, 1937. Xeroxed.

————, and Tree, Roland. "Comparative Cartography Exemplified in an Analytical & Bibliographical Description of Nearly One Hundred Maps and Charts of the American Continent Published in Great Britain during the Years 1600 to 1850." In *Essays Honoring Lawrence C. Wroth,* pp. 305–363. Portland, Me., 1951; reprinted, with addenda, as no. 39 in the Map Collectors' Series. London: Map Collectors' Circle, 1967.

Stevens, Henry, Son & Stiles. "Maps and Plans." In *The American War of Independence: Its History, Origin and Progress as Revealed by Contemporary Books, Pamphlets, Manuscripts, Maps and Plans . . . together with an Introduction by Dr. Randolph G. Adams,* pp. 103–36. London, 1931.

————. *Notes Biographical and Bibliographical on the Atlantic Neptune.* London, 1937.

Stokes, Isaac N. Phelps. *The Iconography of Manhattan Island, 1498–1909. Compiled from Original Sovrces and Illvstrated by Photointaglio Reprodvctions of Important Maps, Plans, Views, and Docvments in Pvblic and Private Collections.* 6 vols. New York: Robert H. Dodd, 1915–28.

Stokes, Isaac N. Phelps, and Haskell, Daniel Carl. *American Historical Prints, Early Views of American Cities, Etc.* New York: New York Public Library, 1932.

Swem, Earl Gregg. *Maps Relating to Virginia in the Virginia State Library and other Departments of the Commonwealth.* Bulletin of the Virginia State Library, vol. 7, nos. 2 & 3. Richmond: Davis Bottom, 1914.

Tarleton, Banastre. *A History of the Campaigns of 1780 and 1781, in the Southern Provinces of North America.* London: T. Cadell, 1787.   60, 83, 90, 92, 197

Thompson, Edmund. *Maps of Connecticut before the Year 1800: A Descriptive List.* Windham, Conn.: Hawthorn House, 1940.

[Tornquist, Carl Gustaf]. *Grefve Grasses siö-batailler, och krigsoperationerne uti Vest-Indien, ifrån början af år 1781 til krigets slut; med dertil hörande historiske anmärkningar.* Stockholm: Joh. Christ. Holmberg, 1787. 158, 162, 168, 169, 170, 171, 172, 183

———. *The Naval Campaigns of Count de Grasse during the American Revolution, 1781–1783.* Translated from the Swedish with Introduction, Notes, and Appendices . . . by Amandus Johnson. Philadelphia: Swedish Colonial Society, 1942.

The Town and Country Magazine; or, Universal Repository of Knowledge, Instruction, and Entertainment. London: A. Hamilton et al., 1769–96. 14

U. S. Navy Dept. *The American Revolution, 1775–1783: An Atlas of 18th Century Maps and Charts.* Compiled by W. Bart Greenwood. Washington: G. P. O., 1972.

The Universal Magazine of Knowledge and Pleasure. London: J. Hinton et al., 1747–1815. 7, 114

Verner, Coolie. "Carto-bibliographical Description: The Analysis of Variants in Maps Printed From Copperplates." *American Cartographer* 1 (1974): 77–87.

———. *Maps of the Yorktown Campaign, 1780–1781: A Preliminary Checklist of Printed and Manuscript Maps Prior to 1800.* Map Collectors' Series, no. 18. London: Map Collectors' Circle, 1965.

Vietor, Alexander O. "The Bauman Map of the Siege of Yorktown." In Yale University Library, *Gazette* 21 (1946): 15–17.

The Virginia Magazine of History and Biography. Richmond: The Virginia Historical Society, 1893– .

Walker's Hibernian Magazine; or, Compendium of Entertaining Knowledge. Dublin: R. Gibson, 1771–1811. 8, 207

[West, Benjamin]. *Bickerstaff's New-England Almanack, for the Year of Our Lord, 1776.* Norwich, Conn.: Robertsons and Trumbull, [1775]. 11

Wheat, James Clements, and Brun, Christian F. *Maps and Charts Published in America Before 1800: A Bibliography.* New Haven: Yale University Press, 1969.

References

Winsor, Justin. "Maps of the Revolutionary Period, Plans of the Battle of Bunker Hill, British Lines on Boston Neck, Maps of Boston Subsequent to the Revolution." In *The Memorial History of Boston, Including Suffolk County, Massachusetts, 1630–1880*, vol. 3, pp. i-xii. Boston: James R. Osgood and Co., 1882.

————, ed. *Narrative and Critical History of America.* 8 vols. Boston and New York: Houghton, Mifflin, 1884–89. Vol. 6, *The United States of North America, Part I*, 1888.

————. *The Reader's Handbook of the American Revolution, 1761–1783.* Boston and New York: Houghton, Mifflin, 1893.

Wymberley Jones De Renne Georgia Library. "Maps and Plans." In *Catalogue of the Wymberley Jones De Renne Georgia Library at Wormsloe, Isle of Hope, near Savannah, Georgia*, vol. 3, pp. 1193–1256. Wormsloe, 1931.

INDEX

Personal and corporate names associated with the production of the maps are printed in SMALL CAPITALS; titles of maps in *italics*; and locations of battles, campaigns, and theaters in roman type. Numbers refer to entries in this bibliography, not pages.